THE

SOLUTION

WITHDRAWN

D0970987

THE

8%

SOLUTION

Preventing Serious,
Repeat Juvenile Crime

Michael Schumacher / Gwen A. Kurz

Sage Publications, Inc.
International Educational and Professional Publisher
Thousand Oaks ▪ London ▪ New Delhi

For information:

Sage Publications, Inc.
2455 Teller Road
Thousand Oaks, California 91320
E-mail: order@sagepub.com

Sage Publications Ltd.
6 Bonhill Street
London EC2A 4PU
United Kingdom

Sage Publications India Pvt. Ltd.
M-32 Market
Greater Kailash I
New Delhi 110 048 India

Printed in the United States of America

Library of Congress Cataloging-in-Publication Data

Schumacher, Michael Allen.
   The 8 % solution: Preventing serious, repeat juvenile crime / by
Michael Schumacher, Gwen A. Kurz.
       p.   cm.
   Includes bibliographical references and index.
   ISBN 0-7619-1790-X (cloth: alk. paper) — ISBN 0-7619-1791-8 (pbk. : alk.
paper)
   1. Juvenile delinquents—Rehabilitation—California. 2. Social
work with juvenile delinquents—California. 3. Juvenile
delinquents—California—Prevention. 4. Juvenile
recidivists—California. 5. Criminal behavior, Prediction of.
I.Kurz, Gwen A. II. Title.
III. Title: 8 percent solution.
HV9105.C2 S38 2000
364.36'0973—dc21   99-050524

This book is printed on acid-free paper.

00   01   02   03   04   05   06   7   6   5   4   3   2   1

Cover design: Len Bertini, President, CPS Digital, Inc.,
                210 East Helen St., Palatine,
                IL 60067

Contents

Dedication

This book is dedicated to the fine men and women of the Orange County Probation Department who labor daily to make Orange County, California, a better, safer place for all of us.

Acknowledgments

All the staff of the Orange County Probation Department deserve praise for the part they played in the development of the 8% Problem research and the subsequent work on the 8% Early Intervention Program. Without their dedicated efforts, none of this would have been possible.

The primary credit for designing and guiding the study goes to Gwen Kurz, the director of program support and research, whose genius was behind the creation of the 8% studies and who continues as principal project investigator. In all phases of the 8% Problem studies, Gwen has been ably assisted by research analyst Lou Moore. Sue Collins, a senior research analyst, has also materially contributed to this venture by helping to develop the strong theoretical base on which the 8% Early Intervention Program is built and by her ongoing efforts to keep the 8% Problem Solution on track.

While the researchers were engaged in documenting the activities of the thousands of juveniles under study, life in probation field casework was under the guidance of Juvenile Supervision Director Bill Brooks, who now superbly oversees 8% Early Intervention Program activities as the director of community programs. The supervisors, counselors, and probation officers who handle the day-to-day casework, as well as our many collaborative partners, cannot be given enough credit for what they have helped us to learn about high-risk youths and families.

Of these individuals, the most significant contributor has been Monica Gallagher. She was the supervising probation officer who directed the 2-year field test of the 8% program model. She guided its transition from a primarily probation-directed intensive supervision program to the integrated, multidisciplinary service delivery system of today, with its impressive array of family-oriented services.

Although a few people were closer to the action than others, the impetus for the 8% studies arose from a strategic planning effort on the part of the probation department begun in 1988, that included all the division directors and chief deputies in determining the future directions for the probation department. It was during this time that the principal research questions were formulated and our plan for the future initiated. Without the support and determination of all these hard-working managers, the study and obviously this book would never have become a reality. We offer them our profound thanks.

This acknowledgment would not be complete without thanking the members of our private sector support group, the Probation Community

Action Association (PCAA), for their dedication to the furtherance of our work. All proceeds from this book will be donated to the PCAA for its ongoing support of the 8% Early Intervention Program.

We owe a great debt of gratitude to Rod Speer, whose creativity and literary style have made this book much more readable. His help was invaluable in researching the anecdotal case examples, providing editorial comments and critique, and putting the finishing touches on the manuscript. Also deserving a round of applause was Mary Krutcik, who had the unenviable task of translating dictation and notes into an acceptable product, and Janice Burke, who proofread the final draft before publication. We thank all of you.

Also we express appreciation to Chief Deputy Probation Officers John Robinson, Stephanie Lewis, and Don Hallstrom and to Division Director Bill Brooks for their final review of the draft of the book to make sure nothing was amiss. Another reviewer of several drafts of the book and technical contributor to the theoretical base of the 8% Early Intervention Program is our friend and colleague James C. "Buddy" Howell. He is the former research director of the federal Office of Juvenile Justice and Delinquency Prevention (OJJDP) and the primary architect of OJJDP's Comprehensive Strategy for Serious, Violent, and Chronic Juvenile Offenders (Wilson & Howell, 1993). His advice and encouragement have been invaluable to us in the continuing research effort.

Finally, we want to thank the past and present boards of supervisors of Orange County, County Executive Officer Jan Mittermeier, and the presiding judges of Orange County Juvenile Court for their guidance, support, and direction during the 7 years of the original 8% studies and during our development of the 8% Early Intervention Program. Without their foresight, this landmark research would not have become a reality.

To all the people already acknowledged and those unsung heroes whose names have been inadvertently overlooked, we believe you can all be very proud of the products derived from the 8% Problem research. The principles underlying the 8% Problem studies and the 8% Early Intervention Program are free for the taking. It is our profound hope that they will be used by communities throughout our great nation to reduce crime, reclaim lives, and make the streets safer for current and future generations. If we are successful in this venture, we have all had a part in making history.

Introduction

As serious juvenile crimes continue to make headlines and the youths who commit them begin their criminal careers earlier in life, cries go out in state legislatures and the halls of Congress for more police on the streets, more jails, and more prisons. Although additional police officers and prisons are needed, they are extremely expensive for society to sustain. They are also "after-the-fact" remedies. Once a criminal has been caught victimizing the community one too many times, society protects itself by paying for months and often years of incarceration.

The 8% Problem studies pave the way for a better long-term solution to serious repeat offending by focusing attention on those young juvenile offenders who are most likely to become the career criminals of tomorrow. This book is about identifying these young people and providing them with individual skill-building and family-oriented services to mitigate the factors that we have determined link kids to serious repeat crime.

Kids who get into trouble repeatedly initially enter the juvenile justice system with a full-blown set of problems that differentiate them from those who get into trouble with the law once, twice, or even three times. These differences are consistent and form a sound basis for identifying high-risk, first-time juvenile offenders so that attention can be focused early on those who most need help. This does not excuse any criminal behavior. It is necessary to hold all young people accountable for criminal offenses through a system of reasonable and graduated sanctions. That should not be the end of it, however.

Some people in criminal justice believe that even if differences do exist among juvenile offenders and can be reliably measured, all young people should still be treated in the same way. They fear that acting on identified differences will result in discrimination or in labeling kids as "losers" destined to be life-long criminals. Certainly, we must be cautious in our approach and consider each youth's rights and needs. In no way should a young person be treated more harshly because of a presumption that he or she will commit additional crimes. Also, neither should any young person be made to feel that a life of crime is his or her inevitable destiny.

We at the Orange County (California) Probation Department, however, believe it is critical to recognize important differences early on and respond accordingly. That response is not to punish a youth for uncommitted crimes, but rather to provide assistance which promotes better parenting and helps youth overcome personal problems associated with serious repeat offending. Even in a worst-case scenario, the targeted kids and families receive more help than they would have otherwise received.

To make a dent in the long-term crime problem, we must determine which young people are most likely to become serious, chronic lawbreakers and focus our intervention efforts on breaking this cycle of crime. This book is the beginning of a road map on how to break this cycle. In it, we have attempted to describe in a readable way a set of characteristics and problems that are far more complicated than they may seem on the surface.

We spent 7 years identifying the 8% risk factors. We spent 5 more years developing and testing early intervention strategies aimed at helping 8% Problem youth and families avoid the pain and lost productivity associated with serious, chronic offending. This has been slow, difficult work. It appears we are on the right track, however.

The theoretical model developed shortly after the 8% Problem study was completed in 1994 has served us very well. As those underlying principles were transformed into a viable, working program, we learned many important lessons worth sharing. Today, we are partners in the 8% Solution with a number of county and private agencies providing an array of program services at Youth and Family Resource Centers throughout Orange County.

Youth in our 8% Solution experiment receive a high level of supervision, structure, and support as they work to build academic and social skills, and overcome addictions and other problems in their lives. In addition, their brothers, sisters, and parents benefit from program services. As a result, the teenagers in the 8% program have committed fewer and less serious offenses and have served less time in custody than their counterparts receiving standard probation services.

As of June 1997, we began testing the 8% Solution using approved scientific methods. While this evaluation will continue until at least June 2001, the preliminary results are promising. The 8% Solution is still a work in progress, yet it is an important work that we believe is well worth continuing. After reading this book, we hope that you agree.

Part I

The 8% Problem

1

The 8% Problem
Serious, Chronic Juvenile Offenders

Orange County, California, is known for tourist attractions such as Disneyland and Knott's Berry Farm, for professional sports teams such as the Anaheim Angels and Anaheim Mighty Ducks, for its moderate Mediterranean climate, for miles of beautiful sandy beaches, and for its affluent suburbs, trendy shopping malls, and modern office complexes of gleaming glass. Like any major metropolitan community, however, it has its share of serious crime and other urban ills.

The major boulevards are home to tourist attractions, but they were also home to a 13-year-old drug-addicted runaway we will call Gina, to protect her identity. She walked a boulevard's "motel row" as a prostitute to eat and to support a $250-a-day cocaine habit. When she was not looking for customers, her "friends" enticed her to steal cars, sometimes several in one night.

Gina's struggle with drug addiction is easy to trace. Her parents introduced her to the fleeting "highs" and years of painful addiction when she was a mere 9-years old. First, her parents smoked marijuana "joints" with her. Later, they used cocaine.

Home life was chaotic. Between violent fights with her mother, Gina bounced from foster home to foster home, and she spent a year in a residential center for juvenile drug addicts. This young lady, initially brought to the attention of the juvenile justice system at age 13, was well on her way toward becoming the "8% Problem" as a serious, chronic juvenile offender. Gina was provided little, if any, chance to avoid a life of crime and addiction. Her life is the formula for disaster for a kid.

Defining the 8% Problem

What are serious, chronic juvenile offenders, and why do we dub them the 8% Problem?[1] This is a shorthand reference to a key finding of a 7-year research study conducted by the Orange County Probation Department on juvenile crime (see Appendix A). The 8% Problem refers to a small percentage of identifiable youth who have been referred to the juve-

nile justice system for crimes a minimum of four times within a 3-year period. They are responsible for the lion's share of the juvenile court's repeat business, particularly that involving serious, repeat crimes.

The probation department serves as the "front door" of the juvenile
justice system in Orange County, which is comprised of 32 cities and 2.7
million people. Probation officers screen an average of 1,000 cases per
month alleging juvenile crimes. These cases are sent to the department
primarily by police agencies for potential handling in Orange County Juvenile Court. Orange County probation officers supervise approximately 7,000
teenagers who have committed crimes. The probation department also
operates five juvenile institutions with approximately 800 beds, including
the county's juvenile hall.

Through the 8% Problem research, we did not seek to test any particular kind of juvenile crime prevention program or technique. We were
simply seeking answers to some basic questions: How effective are we in
preventing a juvenile offender from committing additional crimes? Who do
and who don't we do a good job with? If one can distinguish between
these two groups, how early can one do so? Finally, the $64,000 ques-
tion: Can we turn our "failures" into successes?

To answer these questions, our research staff examined two groups of
first-time offenders, one with 3,304 youths who were charged with crimes
during the first 6 months of 1985 and another with 3,164 juveniles facing
criminal charges in the first 6 months of 1987. All these youth were initially
tracked for 3 years, and representative subsamples were followed for 6
years (see Appendix B).

What our research staff discovered surprises most people. As Table
1.1 shows, the vast majority of these kids (70%) committed just one crime
during the 3-year tracking period. They committed no additional crimes in
Orange County, which the police sought to bring to juvenile court's attention during these 3 years. Something worked in their lives to keep them
out of further trouble. Possibly it was the juvenile justice system, their own
remorse, or the involvement of concerned parents. Another 22% were
accused of one or two more crimes (for a total of two or three crimes)
during the 3-year follow-up period, but their criminal careers also appeared
to end.

In addition, there was this small, but very troublesome, 8%. These
youths, like Gina, were arrested repeatedly. In fact, this 8% of first-time
offenders went on to comprise 55% of our repeat cases. These were the
same names that kept appearing on police reports and juvenile court dock-
ets. They were the same faces that our juvenile hall staff had become
accustomed to seeing. They were the same young people who were victimizing county residents repeatedly, first as juveniles and later as adults.[2]

TABLE 1.1   Orange County Juvenile Justice System Recidivism
Analyses

1985 Initial Referral Group

No. of Referrals per Minor during 3-year Tracking Period	No. of Minors in Each Category	% of Total Minors	No. of Referrals for Each Category	No. of Subsequent Referrals	% of Subsequent Referrals
1	2,190	66	2,190	0	0
2	541	16	1,082	541	22
3	248	8	744	496	20
4-14	325	10	1,771	1,446	58
Total	**3,304**	**100**	**5,787**	**2,483**	**100%**

1987 Initial Referral Group

No. of Referrals per Minor during 3-year Tracking Period	Number of Minors in Each Category	% of Total Minors	No. of Referrals for Each Category	No. of Subsequent Referrals	% of Subsequent Referrals
1	2,234	71	2,234	0	0
2	472	15	944	472	24
3	205	6	615	410	21
4-14	253	8	1,339	1,086	55
Total	**3,164**	**100**	**5,132**	**1,968**	**100%**

Nearly all were found by the court to have committed at least one very serious or violent crime or both.

From our 7-year study, we found that more than half of the 8% Problem kids continued lives of crime as young adults. As Table 1.2 shows, these serious, chronic juvenile offenders were formally handled by Orange County's justice system an average of eight times and served nearly 20 months in adult and juvenile custody facilities in the 6-year follow-up period. These are the kids that concern us deeply, and these are the kids for which we named our study.

The 8% Risk Profile

The fact that a small group of kids are arrested repeatedly is not news in the juvenile justice business. Numerous studies throughout the United States have attested to this fact.[3-8] What is important about the 8% Problem study is gaining an understanding of who these kids are, which is the first step to help solve the problem.

Our research shows that the kids who become the 8% Problem are dramatically different from those youth who are arrested once and do not return to juvenile court. These differences are evident at the first arrest and referral to juvenile court. It is not, as some believe, something which develops after being exposed to the juvenile justice system. There is no doubt that 8% kids do continue to get worse, if no one does anything about the problem. The youth that go on to become serious, chronic juvenile

TABLE 1.2   Results of 6-Year Individual Case Tracking
            for 1987 Subsamples

Six-Year Tracking Measure	Non-Recidivists 1 referral only; (N = 36)	Low-Rate Recidivists 2 or 3 referrals; (N = 58)	Chronic Recidivists 4+ referrals; (N = 77)
Average number of juvenile referrals	1.1	2.4	6.0
Average juvenile commitment time (months)	1.4	1.4	13.9
Percentage with any juvenile commitment	28	47	88
Average number of adult arrests	0.16	0.46	1.7
Average adult commitment time (months)	1.1	1.6 [a]	5.7
Percentage with adult record	6	26	53
Percentage with any adult commitments	6	7	33
Average total juvenile referrals/adult arrests	1.3	2.9	7.7
Average total commitment time (juvenile and adult) (months)	2.5	3.0 [a]	19.6
Percentage with any commitments (juvenile and adult)	31	50	90

offenders enter the system with a complex set of problems that make them much more likely to get into trouble and to stay in trouble.

Risk Factor 1 – Crime at an Early Age

Our 8% Problem studies clearly demonstrate that youth who are age 15 or younger when first referred to juvenile court for criminal behavior are much more likely to become serious, chronic juvenile offenders than those who commit their first crime at age 16 or older. As Table 1.3 indicates, these differences are even greater for those first-time offenders whose initial juvenile court referral results in court wardship and probation supervision.

Risk Factor 2 – Multiproblem Profile

The 8% studies found that in addition to beginning their criminal conduct at a young age, the youth who become chronic juvenile offenders typically display at least three of the problems discussed in the following sections. [9]

Problem 1: Disrupted Families

Eight-percent youth are much more likely to come from a disrupted family. By disrupted, we mean family problems that make life miserable for

TABLE 1.3 Chronic Recidivism Rates by Age of First Juvenile Court Referral -- 1987 Initial Referral Group

All initial referrals	Age 15 or less (N = 849)	Age 16 or older (N = 2,266)	Total Referrals (N = 3,115)
% Total cohort	27	73	100
% Chronic recidivist	17	5	8
All initial referrals resulting in wardship	**Age 15 or less** (N = 221)	**Age 16 or older** (N = 683)	**Total wards** (N = 904)
% Total cohort	24	76	100
% Chronic recidivist	32	8	14

Note: Some possible reasons for the previously noted differences will be explained later. Since 1987, however, we have observed that 8% youth appear to be starting their criminal careers at increasingly younger ages. Nonetheless, the majority are still ages 13 to 15 when initially referred for potential juvenile court handling.

a child, interrupt normal child development, or essentially force children to raise themselves. This could involve conscious neglect or parents so overwhelmed with survival that they cannot or do not adequately structure, supervise, and support their kids. It could be even worse, involving actual physical or sexual abuse by a parent or "significant other" or parents who berate their offspring so badly that it is considered "psychological abuse."

Not surprisingly, many of these youth become runaways. Others try to tough it out. Unfortunately, many slip into criminal behavior and will become the abusive parents or violent offenders of the next generation.

Problem 2: School Failure

Given the previous discussion, it should not be a surprise that another characteristic of this group is failure in school. Interestingly, the majority of 8% kids are still in school when we first come into contact with them. They have not dropped out yet. Most, however, are doing poorly academically, frequently truant, or on suspension for consistently bad behavior. Many have undiagnosed learning disabilities.

They are on the verge of abandoning school to "hang out" with delinquent friends or are one step away from being expelled. They are prime candidates for so-called continuation or juvenile court schools, and they will likely receive most of their remaining education while locked in correctional institutions.

Problem 3: Drug and Alcohol Abuse

A significant proportion of 8% kids are involved from an early age in drug and alcohol abuse. We are not talking about kids who drink an occasional beer or try smoking a marijuana joint at a party. These 8% potential youth are on the road to becoming regular users and abusers. It is part of their life, often used to hide from reality by masking pain, humiliation, degradation, or boredom. Sadly, illegal drugs and alcohol are far too readily available for children, as is tobacco, the most frequent gateway drug for young people. Sadder still is the fact that parents are often totally unaware of this problem or are "in denial" regarding the drug or alcohol abuse in their own lives.

Problem 4: Predelinquent Behaviors (Gang Ties, Running Away, and Stealing)

The final characteristic separating potential chronic juvenile offenders from their less delinquent counterparts is a composite "predelinquency" factor, so named by our research staff because it includes behavior highly associated with later delinquency and serious chronic offending.

The first of these behaviors is gang association. In 1987, surprisingly few 8% youth (16%) identified themselves as gang members at the time of their first arrest. However, their "partners in crime" were often gang members based on police reports or their own admissions. Annual surveys of the Orange County kids in custody show that approximately two thirds of these more criminally sophisticated youth are significantly involved in gangs. It appears that many potential 8% youth are at an important crossroads when we in probation first see them, and that too many perceive gangs as their only route to success, acceptance, and relative safety. We may have only a short window in time to change this perception, and assist youth in identifying viable alternatives.

The second predelinquent measure is chronic runaway behavior. Again, although seemingly involving a small proportion of potential 8% youth, our studies indicate that we need to pay close attention to such behavior on the part of children and adolescents. Repeatedly running away is closely associated with physical, sexual, and emotional abuse. Most youth "run" for a reason. We must look to the underlying causes for the solution and be cautious about forcing kids back into potentially harmful situations without adequate intervention and protection.

The final part of the predelinquency risk factor is a pattern of stealing. These are the kids who become known for taking anything that is not "nailed down," from "disappearing" lunch money at school to "stuff" missing from a neighbor's garage and "joyriding" in someone else's car. Such actions are indicative of kids who are more needy emotionally than monetarily and who steal to get attention. It works well, too, except for the negative consequences.

What do all these kids have in common? The longer these behaviors continue, the more socially isolated such youth become. They not only hang with the "wrong crowd" but also are the wrong crowd. These youth have too much time on their hands, too little supervision, and too much reinforcement for bad behavior. Hanging out may also involve smoking cigarettes, drinking alcohol, using drugs, engaging in sex, shoplifting, and committing daytime burglaries.

The previous sections discussed the characteristics that distinguish youths who are more likely to fall into a cycle of crime from those who are not. What does one do with this information? It seems that it should be a fairly simple matter to select the kids with the characteristics predictive of repeat offending and do something with them. The truth is that the current juvenile justice system is not designed to do this. The system is focused more on the kinds of crimes kids commit rather than on who commits them.

Equal Treatment = Unequal Results

Our system of justice and "fair play" dictates that everyone who commits a similar offense should be treated equally. The juvenile court system is set up this way. Prosecutors and defense attorneys expect it. The difficulty is that a minor's crimes often do not accurately reflect the degree of problems underlying the behavior. We are not saying that some lightweight offenses should be treated with harsh punishment or vice versa. We believe that the juvenile justice system should not overlook a young, first-time offender simply because of the youth's age and the relatively lightweight nature of the offense. This youth could be headed down a long dark path, one littered with crime and innocent victims. This could be a potential "8 percenter."

Consider, for example, the case of two hypothetical teenage boys, John and Rudy. They both run from a liquor store with six-packs of beer, only to fall into the waiting arms of store security staff. Both are ordered by the court to pick up trash for 10 weekends as their punishment. So long as this is done, their relationship with juvenile court concludes until the next offense, if there is one.

Rudy is a potential 8 percenter, whereas John is not. John's family is outraged by his behavior and takes appropriate steps to deal with it, restricting him to home for weeks and taking away television privileges. John is embarrassed by the whole episode and never again steps over the line of criminal behavior.

Rudy's problems, however, are much larger than stealing a six-pack of beer. The weekend trash duty will not turn him around. He ditches school, abuses drugs, and hangs around with other kids who do the same. His parents have little or no impact on his life, so there is no "righting of the ship" after his first brush with the law.

The juvenile justice system may not pay much attention to Rudy until crime number three or four, unless he seriously victimizes someone. By then, however, bad habits have been formed. It is often much too late.

Notes

1.   Kurz, G. A. and Moore, L. E. (1994). "The 8% problem": Chronic juvenile offender recidivism. Santa Ana, CA. Orange County Probation Department.

2.   Only alleged offenses deemed serious enough by local police to be referred to the juvenile justice system in Orange County for potential juvenile court handling were counted in the initial recidivism analyses (Table 1.1). Thus, a youth "cited and released" by a local police agency or arrested in another county would not have been counted. During the 6-year follow-up, however, when adult arrest data became available, it was possible to obtain system data on the handling of criminal complaints from other California counties and other states. All youth who turned age 18 were followed-up as adults in both the 3- and the 6-year tracking efforts.

3.   Wolfgang, M. E., Figlio, R. M. & Sellin, T. (1972). Delinquency in a birth cohort. Chicago: University of Chicago Press.

4.   Wolfgang, M. E., Thornberry, T. P. & Figlio, R. M. (1987). From boy to man, from delinquency to crime. Chicago: University of Chicago Press.

5.   Strasburg, P. (1978). Violent delinquents. New York: Monarch Press.

6.   Hamperin, D., Schuster, R., Dinitz, S., & Conrad, J. (1978). The violent few, a study of dangerous juvenile offenders. Lexington, MA: Lexington Books.

7.   Shannon, L. (1988). Criminal career continuity: Its social context, New York: Human Sciences Press.

8.   Huizinga, D., Loeber, R. & Thornberry, T. (1993). Urban delinquency and substance abuse. Washington, D.C.: U.S. Department of Justice, Office of Juvenile Justice and Delinquency Prevention.

9.   The original 8% Problem study focused on identifying youth at high risk of becoming serious, chronic offenders at the probation intake level (or based on the first or second system referral). The criterion used was two or more 8% risk factors. The work done during the ensuing 5 years focused on the first-time ward population and resulted in refining the multiproblem profile definition to require three or more problems. This change is primarily the result of improved front-end assessment procedures that provide better information on which to base our initial risk assessment and program assignment decisions.

2

Crime at an Early Age
"Let's Give 'Em a Break"

Most people are surprised to learn that whether or not kids are placed on probation "first thing out of the chute," those who begin committing crimes at age 15 or younger are three or four times more likely to become chronic juvenile offenders than those who begin offending as older teenagers. The greatest differences are among those declared "wards of the court" because the seriousness of their crimes and potential threat to public safety warrant direct court involvement through supervision and interventions provided by the probation department. First-time wards are more likely to be burglars, auto thieves, and assailants rather than shoplifters and graffiti vandals, or they may have played a relatively minor role in a more serious crime engineered by older, more criminally sophisticated "friends."

Our researchers tracked a structured subsample of the 1987 first referrals for an additional 3 years, at which time most study cases were well beyond 18 years of age (i.e., 6 years after their first arrest resulting in a juvenile court case). Most of the one-time only offenders who were crime-free as juveniles continued to be crime-free as young adults. In contrast, half of the 8% repeat offenders, typically younger at their first referral, continued the cycle of criminality into their adult years.

Why would the age of first-time offenders play such an important role in how often they reoffend? The primary difference was that most of the teenagers who started their criminal careers at a later age had fewer of the problems that distinguish the 8% repeat offenders. Also, those problems they did have were less severe than those of the younger 8% group. Table 2.1 demonstrates how the number of problem variables differed with the age of the offender, most significantly among those who became serious, chronic juvenile offenders.

There is another reason for the difference, however — one deeply embedded in the way the juvenile justice system treats younger kids. Those kids who need supportive intervention most in their lives, who are at greatest risk for becoming chronic offenders, often receive the least attention from the criminal justice system until after they have established a record of serious repeat offending.

TABLE 2.1   Average Number of Significant Risk Factors
              by Age and Number of Criminal Referrals:
              1987 Initial Referral Cohort Subsamples

Age	Nonrecidivists 1 Referral Only; (N = 36)	Low-Rate Recidivist 2 to 3 Referrals (N = 58)	Chronic Recidivist 4+ Referrals (N = 77)	Total Study Sample (N = 171)
15 or younger	1.27	2.16	3.74	3.01
16 or older	0.96	1.54	2.39	1.64

When younger juveniles (age 15 or younger) are first arrested, there is a tendency for police, prosecutors, defense attorneys, probation officers, and the courts to treat these youth differently than when older youth are involved. Although there are occasional 14-year-old gang shooters, they are the exception and not the rule. Among younger minors, the first offense is commonly lightweight, such as shoplifting or stealing a bicycle. The juvenile justice system is inclined to give young kids a break. We are less sympathetic with kids who are 16 years old or older, even if it is their first offense.

Being given a "break" at this juncture is no break at all for the potential chronic youthful offender. To avoid a cycle of criminality, it is imperative to exact a swift and a sure punishment for each offense and to reduce the number and severity of problems that plague 8% youth and families. Typically, the young first-time offender faces a neither swift nor sure punishment. Furthermore, the family has already demonstrated its inability to solve other problems without help.

Without prompt intervention, we can expect such youth to continually return to court charged with new offenses. It is often not until offense number three or four, at age 16 or older, that the juvenile justice system takes a hard look at the young person and imposes more serious sanctions and closer supervision. By that time, the youth may have dropped out of school, joined a gang, become addicted to drugs, and adopted other bad habits. It may still not be too late to change the behavior, but the prospects for success have certainly diminished, whereas the costs to successfully intervene will have skyrocketed.

By no means do we advocate that a first-time offender fitting the 8% risk profile be treated more harshly than other first-time offenders who face similar criminal charges. A certain standard of justice should prevail, no matter who commits the crime. It is, however, necessary to identify causes of antisocial behavior and address them as early as possible, or expect to pay the consequences later.

For example, consider the case of an innocent-looking 11-year-old girl we'll call Susan, who came to the court's attention for playing with fire outside her home in an upscale neighborhood. Susan and a 7-year-old girlfriend were lighting dry weeds and grass with a cigarette lighter and then stomping out the flames with their feet, until one fire got out of control. Fortunately, fire crews extinguished the fire before it became a raging inferno that could have threatened more people and homes. This is a girl who is still in the sixth grade of elementary school, receives good grades, and lives in a good neighborhood. It would be natural to let her slip through the juvenile justice system with a good lecture about the dangers of playing with fire.

A closer examination, however, reveals that Susan's home life is chaotic. She suffers from depression and is considered suicidal. She was removed from her home at age 10 to live, first, in a county children's home and, later, in a foster home because her stepfather was physically abusive and her mother, a recovering alcoholic, was deemed "unfit."

Susan also exhibits a pattern of stealing. Although no charges were filed, her mother contends that Susan rifled through approximately 50 neighborhood mailboxes looking for credit cards and checks. She was also "along for the ride" when her older half-brother stole a truck. Although very young, Susan abuses alcohol and smokes pot regularly, acts that counselors say are her way of coping with depression over her troubled home life. Susan needs more than a stern lecture. She and her family need serious intervention to prevent her from galloping down the road to a life of crime.

The importance of age at the first offense cannot be overstated. Our 8% Problem studies show that the kids who become serious repeat offenders are not only referred on criminal charges at a young age but also typically enter the juvenile justice system with a set of serious problems that demand attention. These are not problems that develop after the first referral. They are already present, and they will become worse without attention.

It may seem a little backwards to think that an older youth is less likely to become a serious, long-term offender than a younger one. It must be remembered, however, that there is a difference between a youth who starts offending at age 13 and by age 16 is committing serious offenses and a youth whose first offense occurs at age 16 or older. Think of it this way: If Johnny gets into trouble with the law for the first time at age 16 or 17, he has had a longer time to be law-abiding and prosocial than his younger counterpart. What has happened in life to propel him into criminal behavior has been resisted for a longer time. Perhaps parents were there to guide him for some time. Even just a few years seems to have an effect.

Older teenagers commit more serious crimes than do younger offenders. This may be attributable to the fact that they have more opportunities to get into more trouble. They are the ones with greater access to cars, money, and the opposite sex and who have gained more independence from their parents. As with younger minors, however, the severity of the offense is not a good predictor of future offenses; it is the number and severity of 8% risk factors in their lives that make the difference.

The 8% Problem research is a road map. It indicates where one has to go to find kids most in need of help. If we do not follow it, then as a society we will continue to pay the price in terms of wasted lives and unnecessary victims.

3

Disrupted Families
The Continuing Family Crisis

There is an enormous amount of political rhetoric associated with what the "ideal" family should be. We do not re-open that debate here. Certainly, a two-parent family with concerned, loving parents is most desirable. For whatever reasons, however, that is not reality for many American children. Children frequently find themselves in one-parent homes, foster homes, or being raised by relatives or guardians. It appears to be less critical who raises a child than how and in what environment.

Every young person needs the structure, supervision, and support of responsible, caring adults. We call these elements the "three 'S's," and our studies have found that these factors are sorely lacking in 8% families. By structure, we are referring to order and a consistent positive direction in a young person's life. Youth should know what is expected: when to awaken to go to school, when and where to do homework, who is acceptable to "hang out with," what is acceptable to watch on television or at a movie, what time to be home for dinner, how late they can stay out on school nights and weekends, and rules on how to disagree without being disagreeable or violent. This structure not only directs children toward prosocial behavior but also protects them from harm.

All the structure in the world, however, is of little value without "supervision," the effective enforcement of those rules and values. This includes positive reinforcement for rules obeyed, such as rewards and praise, and laying down appropriate consequences for youth who knowingly and deliberately violate rules set up for their benefit. Likewise, it is important for parents to model good behavior. Kids watch to see if what adults say matches what they do.

Parents and guardians also need to provide "support" for the children under their guidance. This means they need to create a nurturing environment that will allow structure and supervision to be maintained. For example, children cannot be expected to give their best effort in school if they arrive there cold, hungry, or sleepy. They cannot be expected to complete homework without a quiet place to concentrate away from a blaring television, or without some help in subjects that are difficult for them. They cannot be expected to obey a curfew if there is no one home to verify it or to receive a call that they may be late. They need healthy alternatives to hanging out with the wrong crowd, such as sports or boys' and girls' clubs. They also need love, positive rewards, and a sense of belonging, all of which should be found in the home environment.

Children learning to adapt in the world simply cannot develop normally or acquire the life skills they need to compete amid chaos, fear, and stress. Some homes have become virtual physical or emotional battlegrounds. In others, the family's energy and resources are focused entirely on survival, such as putting food on the table that day and paying the next month's rent. Unfortunately, this is what the kids in 8% families often deal with on a daily basis.

In the 8% Problem studies, we identified "disrupted families" as a key predictor, if not the single most important predictor, of chronic juvenile crime. In general, there was an overall lack of family structure, supervision, and support mentioned earlier. Specifically, we examined three problem indicators, any of which would categorize a youth as having a disrupted family.

Problem Indicator #1:
Poor Parental Structure and Supervision

This problem stems from many sources. A common denominator is that parents or guardians do not have the slightest idea where their kids go, what they are doing, and whom they are doing "it" with. Eight percent parents have little, if any, positive influence on their children's behavior. The children have learned that they do not need to pay attention to what their parents say because they do not consistently enforce the rules. In a lesser number of cases, control is too high and not appropriate for the age of the child. Hence, kids rebel and reject the parent's authority altogether.

Respect for authority is learned. Rarely will children blindly accept the rules and values set forth by their parents without testing or challenging them. An authority figure who fails to uphold reasonable rules and expectations for behavior will soon discover that he or she is being ignored. What is wanted is what psychologists call "the internalization" of the authority figure's rules and values. When a child internalizes, he or she will accept the parents' values and seek to behave in ways that please them. Likewise, if no one seems to care, or if parental rules and values are unreasonable or inconsistently enforced, they will be rejected and replaced by another set that better meets the child's needs. For teens, this is often the rules and values of a peer group, a very powerful force in the lives of most adolescents.

The efforts of a grandmother raising twin 15-year-old grandsons demonstrate the importance of consistent parental supervision. This grandmother cooperated with the probation department in stopping their drug abuse by ensuring that the twins were regularly tested for drugs at a probation field office. She refused to acknowledge that these teenagers were gang members, however, even though they dressed like gang members, adopted gang nicknames, admitted in letters that they participated in gangs, and were often found associating with a gang some distance away from their middle class neighborhood. She allowed the youths to stay out past their court-imposed 8 p.m. curfew, to continue to wear baggy pants and other identifiable gang clothing, and to continue to hang out with questionable associates. Had the grandmother been more assertive, perhaps the twins would not be, as of this writing, serving time for criminal offenses. In her defense, she was at least trying to raise children whose parents had already "dropped the ball."

Significant, unanticipated events can also abruptly change and seriously alter the course of what had previously been a close-knit, nurturing family. Two of the biggest challenges facing American families are the loss of the primary bread-winner's job, creating serious financial problems, and the emotional upheaval resulting from divorce, which may include a series of stepdads, stepmoms, or "live-ins." These problems often occur simultaneously and create havoc in the life of a child, undermining the emotional support needed for normal child development. It is impossible for a child to form stable, long-term relationships with adults who come and go in their lives or with those who simply have no time or emotional energy left to invest in them.

Such family crises can also be triggered when a parent or family member is seriously ill, dies, or becomes addicted to drugs or alcohol. Family members may be so overcome by grief or consumed with attending to the needs of a particular child or parent that they cannot function properly. For some kids, this can lead to clinical depression. For others, the inability to deal effectively with the grief or loss of parental support and attentiveness results in bottled-up anger that is expressed in inappropriate and sometimes violent ways.

Consider, for example, the family stresses in the life of 15-year-old "Andrew." His mother has a history of alcohol and drug abuse and suffers from depression. "Home" at Christmas was a single room in a low-rent motel, at which there was no play area for kids and no outside greenery – nothing but a black asphalt parking lot.

Andrew shunned his stepfather that Christmas not because he was mean or abusive but out of resignation that he, like the four stepfathers before him, would drift out of Andrew's life as quickly as he drifted in. Andrew had become very close to Stepdad No. 3 only to be crushed when he walked out of their lives, never to return. Andrew was correct about Stepdad No. 5. Within days after Christmas, he and Andrew's mother parted company.

With a shattered home life lacking in structure, supervision, and support, Andrew began turning as early as age 8 to illicit drugs as an escape. Without intervention in his life and that of his family, it would not be surprising for Andrew to end up where his 16 year-old brother is currently – serving an extended sentence in a state juvenile institution, the teenage equivalent of state prison.

Problem Indicator 2: Child Neglect and Abuse

Child neglect can be a chronic condition or one triggered by catastrophic events such as those previously discussed. In either case, intervention is required to avoid or help remove the emotional damage that inevitably leads to a child's dysfunctional behavior. Even when the neglect is unintentional, such as when a parent is consumed with working to put food on the table, children still suffer abandonment and loss. They will not receive the nurturing and guidance needed for sound development.

It is understood that children deprived of food, clothing, or shelter suffer both physically and psychologically. The significant impact of emotional deprivation on a young person's development is less often recognized, however. Kids can survive without many things in a physical sense with minimal damage to their self-esteem. When also deprived of adequate protection, guidance, and emotional support, however, children and adolescents often lose the will to succeed.

Like prolonged neglect, child abuse is a pernicious destroyer of a child's chances for a decent life. If the most important people in a child's life, the parents, think of their child as no more than an object to be exploited or as a whipping post to vent rage, it can be particularly devastating to the child's self-esteem and perspective on human relations. Tragically, many of these child victims grow up with a skewed view of how adults treat children and they themselves pass on a legacy of abuse and neglect to their children. All too often, abusive parents were themselves abused as children. At the very least, kids growing up in abusive homes or circumstances view the world as a hardened, uncaring, and dangerous place. There is ample criminal justice research demonstrating that abuse breeds further abuse and violence begets violence.[1-4]

A recent publication of the U.S. Office of Juvenile Justice and Delinquency Prevention (OJJDP)[5] explores the connections between childhood maltreatment and subsequent problem behaviors based on longitudinal studies conducted in Rochester, New York, Denver, Colorado, and Pittsburgh, Pennsylvania. The researchers for OJJDP's Program of Research on the Causes and Correlates of Delinquency interviewed 4,000 youth at regular intervals for more than a decade. This publication focuses on how maltreated youth differ from the general population in a variety of ways, including serious delinquency and violence. This research clearly shows that mistreating a child significantly increases the chances that a youth will be involved in serious delinquency, and that the more serious the abuse or other maltreatment, the higher the risk for more serious and violent acts.

Research on the effects of childhood trauma on brain development indicates that children who are abused, neglected, or both, particularly in the first 33 months of life, may suffer irreversible consequences. These children can find it extremely difficult to establish meaningful relationships. In addition, the fear they experienced when abused or exposed to continuing domestic violence can linger for years after the fact. As these children grow older, these conditions appear to increase the potential for violent behavior.[6]

One young man, "Gary," was abused, neglected, and abandoned by his parents at an early age. He was practically raised in foster homes and county juvenile institutions. Gary's dad walked out on the family when he was an infant, and his mother sexually molested Gary before he was old enough to go to school. While in institutions, Gary was suicidal, violent, and destructive. He assaulted other kids and staff, and he broke furniture.

While he lived in a foster home, his mother disappeared. For 6 years, he did not know where she was, but he held onto the hope that she would reappear and he could begin a normal life with her. When probation finally caught up with her in another state, she wanted nothing to do with Gary. Needless to say, he was crushed. His inner rage against the world only intensified. Gary was headed down a path that could lead to even more than just chronic criminality; it may render him a true menace to society.

Problem Indicator 3: Criminal Family Members

For some kids, wanting "to grow up to be like mommy or daddy" would mean following in their parents' criminal footsteps. It is not surprising that an 8% youth named "Danny" does not think that spray painting graffiti is a big deal or that his two sisters, ages 9 and 15, have little remorse for being caught shoplifting. That is nickel-and-dime stuff compared to the crimes committed by their dad, who spent most of their childhood in state prison for armed robbery and nearly killing an armored car driver. Danny's mother divorced his father when he went to prison and is now divorcing Danny's stepfather. A husky 5'8" eighth grader, Danny yearns for a father figure in his life. That is why, his mother explains, he tends to hang out with older boys and young men, including the graffiti "taggers" he hooked up with before being placed on probation.

Sometimes, an older brother or sister is involved with criminal street gangs or has a criminal record and encourages the younger sibling to get involved. One young junior high girl on probation learned just how dangerous this can be. She was riding in a car with her boyfriend and with her older brother, a gang member. Shots rang out, and she was hit in the head with a bullet meant for her brother. After struggling on the brink of death for days, she made an amazing recovery from this injury during the following year. Her boyfriend also suffered serious injuries, but recovered.

Family members who shuttle back and forth between home and prison, jail, or juvenile hall can be very disruptive. They send a powerful message to a child that it is okay to disrespect the law and the rights of other people, and that stints behind bars are "normal." We have also learned that these same children are at much greater risk for both abuse and neglect, which makes these "children of offenders" perhaps the most significant in the 8% risk group.

Throughout history, the family has provided the foundation for a child's development of trust, values, and a sense of belonging. The 8% families have serious obstacles, which hinder a child's normal development and open the door to criminal behavior. Some family problems are transient, providing "a light at the end of the tunnel." Other problems, such as Gary's, are more deep-rooted and require extensive long-term help.

Without the needed structure, supervision, and support in their lives, children will test limits where there are none and finally set their own. They will seek a sense of belonging wherever they can find it, which can very well be in the wrong places. They develop a behavioral system embodied in the statement, "I guess it really doesn't matter what I do." Whether parents are unwilling or unable to provide the three S's, the resulting damage is the same and equally disastrous.

The dysfunctional family is such a significant predictor of repeat criminal behavior that many other problems, such as drug abuse, failure in school, and running away from home, could find their origin there. To truly make an impact on the 8% Problem, it is critical to find effective ways of empowering family units and producing a healthier home environment for each child's growth and development.

Notes

1.   Loeber, R., & Stouthamer-Loeber, M. (1986). Family factors as correlates and predictors of juvenile conduct problems and delinquency. In N. Morris & M. Tonry, (Eds.), <u>Crime and justice: Annual review of research</u>. Chicago: University of Chicago Press.

2.   Minty, B. (1988). Public care or distorted family relationships: The antecedents of violent crime. <u>Howard Journal</u>, <u>27</u>(3), 172-187.

3.   McCord, J. (1991). Family relationships, juvenile delinquency, and adult criminality. <u>Criminology</u>, <u>29</u>(3), 557-580.

4.   Wright, K., & Wright, K. (1992). <u>Family life and delinquency and crime: A policymakers' guide to the literature.</u> Washington, DC: U.S. Department of Justice, Office of Juvenile Justice and Delinquency Prevention.

5.   Kelly, B., Thornberry, T. & Smith, C. (1997). <u>In the wake of childhood maltreatment</u>. Washington, DC: U.S. Department of Justice, Office of Juvenile Justice and Delinquency Prevention.

6.   Children's Institute International (CII) Forum (1999, Winter). <u>Early childhood and brain development. CII speaks with Dr. Bruce Perry and Robin Karr-Morse regarding the damage of abuse and neglect.</u> Los Angeles.

4

School Failure

School's Out for Good ... and That's Bad!

We have established that 8% kids are multiproblem youth from multiproblem families. Hence, it is no wonder that with all the difficulties in their lives, many also struggle in school. It would be amazing if they did not. Not uncommonly, these kids skip classes, are frequently absent, or ditch school entirely. When they are in school, they are the ones acting up and starting trouble. They are also the kids who get suspended or expelled and fail multiple subjects. Often, school becomes just another failure in their lives.

Problem Indicator 1: Truancy

Attending school regularly and doing well in school has the same social implications for a kid as having a job does for an adult. Consider one of the very first questions adults in our culture ask one another after meeting: "What do you do?" In some cultures, people would look at the questioner with a blank expression and respond, "What do I do *what*?" In our culture, it is understood that the question means "How do you earn a living?" The social implications are vastly different for responses such as "I am a medical doctor" and "I am unemployed and haven't worked for years." There is either respect and admiration for someone holding a prestigious professional occupation or underlying doubts about one's lack of skills or motivation.

Holding a job in our society is more than simply earning money to pay for basic necessities. It is a measure of who we are as individuals. Regardless of the kind of work done, it is important for self-esteem to be employed. It is difficult in our society to have self esteem or earn the respect of others without a job unless one is truly unable to hold a job.

Similarly, attending school has the same effect on self-esteem for youth. Children gain it from attending school and much more so from succeeding in school. It is the place where children get to test their mental and social abilities. The experience can be very positive or deflating for young, tender egos.

Children also learn much about how to relate to the world, to its organizations, and to the whole idea of work through the regimen of school. Consider the similarities between an adult who gets ready for work in the morning, gets prepared for the day's events, and travels many miles to spend the day working with others and a child's preparation for the school day.

Children similarly have their first experiences with waking up on time, getting ready for the day, leaving the house on time, being prepared with their homework, and participating in joint activities with their peers in the school setting. Clearly, in addition to becoming educated, a whole set of work ethics is being developed. How well juveniles learn these lessons will determine in some measure how well they will perform in school and can influence their entire lives.

Being successful in class, getting praise from a teacher, and eventually graduating all help children understand how to accomplish tasks and achieve success. Doing poorly in school or missing the experience altogether through truancy has the opposite effect. It leaves kids ill prepared to compete in a complex society in which education and a work ethic are essential to getting and holding a decent job.

Many potential 8% youth do not receive much support from home to attend school on a regular basis due to several factors. One is the generally chaotic nature of their homes. Parents have difficulty organizing their own lives to get to work or other appointments and frequently just do not wake kids up in time to catch the school bus. On days when they are able to obtain work, some parents keep youth of junior high or high school age at home to watch younger siblings.

Still others, having not been successful in educational pursuits themselves, see little value in formal education beyond elementary school. They would prefer these youth seek employment, even at menial jobs, to assist in supporting the family. A small proportion of 8% kids move so frequently that there are significant lapses in their attendance due to the requirements to reenroll at a new school.

Whatever the reasons, at the point that 8% minors fall sufficiently behind in their schooling to receive failing grades, they begin to dislike or devalue school attendance. Most will not attribute the reasons for their lack of success to their parents or the lack of appropriate educational interventions. They just feel plain stupid and want to do something else, anything that will make them feel better about themselves. Often, this is just staying at home or hanging out with other truants on the street. We should not be fooled, however. These kids are still learning. They are not learning anything that will help them to succeed in our increasingly complex and competitive world, however.

Problem Indicator 2:
School Suspension, Expulsion, or Botl

Although some 8% kids "drop out" when they begin experiencing academic problems or feel increasingly unable to cope with problems at school or at home, others "act out." They are angry at the hand life has dealt them. They seek the attention at school they believe they are unable to get at home. The attention they receive is, by and large, negative.

Teachers or guidance counselors who seek to help by working with the family are often "turned off" or turned away by parents who have little desire or insight into how to correct these problems. This speaks again to the multiproblem nature of 8% families. Few school programs have anything approaching the intervention resources that are needed to effectively deal with these problems.

As the youth's frustration and acting out behavior escalates, school officials revert to either isolating such kids in classrooms devoted to "problem" youth or, as last resorts, school suspensions and expulsions. Their need to maintain order and protect the safety of the majority of prosocial kids takes precedence over their desire to work with such troubled youth. This is not an indictment of our educational system but rather a statement of the realities of urban life in America today.

The net result, at best, is that 8% youth stay in school but miss out on many of the positive attributes of being in the mainstream educational track. They are exposed to fewer opportunities for enrichment or advancement and exposed to more poor role models. Typically, they very quickly join their truant peers "on the street" in search of some form of positive self-esteem. Too often, participation in crime, whether with gangs or on an individual basis, earns them the status that they could not find in school.

Problem Indicator 3: Failing Grades

Many youth may at one time or another encounter coursework or have personality conflicts with a particular teacher that result in a failing grade. They typically receive tutoring or make up coursework after school or during summer vacation. This is not the problem indicator to which we refer.

Eight-percent youth generally fail courses in several subject areas. They may have missed large blocks of instruction, lack parental support to achieve academically, have undiagnosed learning disabilities, have untreated emotional or developmental problems that further interfere with their ability to learn, or have a combination of problems hindering them.

The Risk and Needs Assessment data gathered by the probation department on new juvenile probationers since the mid-1980s indicates that both low-rate and chronic juvenile offenders have a higher incidence of diagnosed learning disabilities (20 to 22%) than youth with just one probation referral for a crime (2 to 4%). In addition, our work with the 8% Early Intervention Program, particularly since the program has included medical and mental health assessments, revealed that 8% youth also have a much higher incidence of developmental and emotional problems. These include clinical depression, attention deficit disorder, attention deficit hyperactivity disorder, post-traumatic stress disorder, and other conduct disorders that were previously undiagnosed.

We discovered that developmental learning and related mental health problems in particular differentiate 8% potential youth from those who do not become chronic offenders. Assessments conducted by our local chapter of the American Academy of Pediatrics (AAP) during the field test of the 8% Early Intervention Program alerted us to this fact. Both the AAP study of 40 field test youth and their siblings and the mental health assessments of all experimental program youth conducted since June 1998 indicate that at least half suffer from developmental learning and mental health problems. Given the higher incidence of abuse, neglect, and family violence documented for 8% youth and families, many of these problems may have originated in early childhood trauma. This finding can help educators and case staff to develop the educational and treatment strategies that 8% youth will likely need to overcome learning difficulties.

Most youth who do not become chronic offenders are able to learn in traditional ways. If not, their parents ensure that they receive specialized help. In contrast, 8% kids generally do not have the benefit of informed parents who are effective advocates for their special needs, nor are they generally in school long enough in one place for teachers to recognize the problem. If learning disabilities and related developmental or emotional problems are not diagnosed and treated by the time minors reach junior high school, it is unlikely that they ever will be, because minors spend less time with any one teacher and fall increasingly behind.

The experience of a young 8% teenager, "Julio," demonstrates a typical 8% case example. Sadly, Julio builds his self-esteem on the streets, not in school. He is a poor reader and a special education student who never did well in school. Julio was expelled from two traditional junior high schools for poor behavior, rules infractions, and fighting. When he was caught carrying a screwdriver "for protection," he was expelled from a special continuation school, which in California often serves as a last chance for students who cannot make it in their regular neighborhood schools.

Now 15, he gets a thrill from looking intimidating and not from making "A"s or "B"s. He struts down the sidewalk with a shaved head, wearing baggy pants and sunglasses, and says he enjoys watching others cross the street to avoid him. School, he says, is "boring." He does not see a point to it.

Look at Julio's role models. He is the only child of a mother who once served time in a federal prison for stealing mail. He never knew his father. He has one uncle in state prison and another in an outlaw motorcycle gang. Julio is headed down a path similar to the one that the adults in his life have followed.

He has learned skills, but not ones that endear him to law-abiding citizens. He learned to break into cars at age 8 and prides himself on how quickly and efficiently he can do so and drive away without the keys. His small arms, he noted, were ideal for slipping through slightly opened windows to unlock cars.

Kids who fall into the potential 8% group cannot afford to hang out as Julio does with fellow gang members in his neighborhood. When they do, they get into trouble. Negative influences begin to dominate their lives. Youth such as Julio need to be in school and have a positive direction in life, aiming for further education or job skills.

It is important to note that the 8% repeat offenders from our study were generally still in school at the time of their initial brush with the law. Also, they were still in their own neighborhood school, as opposed to a court school or alternative educational setting. They were not necessarily doing very well academically, but they had not dropped out yet. Unfortunately, once having achieved 8% problem status, most were finished with school for good.

It is critical that high-risk youth either stay in their own school or enroll in an alternative one that will help them to learn not only academics but also the skills and values needed to be successful in adult endeavors. This will not occur without accurate early assessment of the developmental or emotional problems or both that may contribute to each minor's unique learning difficulties.

Note

1.   Stewart, D., (1996), <u>The 8% solution: Medical intervention</u> (CATCH planning grant final report). American Academy of Pediatrics, Orange, CA.

5

Drug and Alcohol Abuse
Getting "High" and Sinking Low

Illegal drugs, and the abuse of legal ones, have plagued our society for decades. Worse is that drugs and alcohol have become readily available to children. Kids get involved with drugs and alcohol for a variety of reasons. Some are influenced by peer pressure, "because everyone else is doing it," and use drugs and alcohol as a potentially dangerous form of recreation and entertainment. Others consider it more adult-like. On occasion, it is an experiment that gets out of hand. For the 8% youngster, it can also be a remedy to cope with the very real problems of life, a means to medicate against emotional pain.

Adolescence produces plenty of stress and burdens on all youth. With the competitive nature of American society and all of its demands, drugs and alcohol seem to be an easy way to "get away from it all." That is, until reality comes crashing back. For the high-risk youth with whom we work, reality is often not a pretty picture. They may have been abandoned by a parent, be failing in school, face abuse in the home, or live amid extreme poverty and violence in their neighborhood. It is little wonder that the escape offered by drugs and alcohol provides such an allure for these youngsters.

Children cannot function in school or in society while under the influence. Drugs and alcohol inhibit learning. They prevent young people from gaining the skills and information necessary to make a living and survive in a complex society. They are also a stumbling block to establishing values important to good citizenship and accepting the responsibilities of an adult.

In our study, drug and alcohol abuse were identified as equivalent problems, each contributing to a much higher risk of chronic juvenile offending for first-time wards age 15 and younger when two or more additional 8% risk factors were present. As an individual 8% risk factor, it does not appear to matter much which kind of chemical interferes with the function and development of kids. Some are just more dangerous than others.

For a youngster we will name Ricky, drugs were as close as his neighborhood park. He was a 12-year-old sixth grader when he walked into the park and first saw a friend smoking pot with much older boys. That day would forever change Ricky's life, sending it into a downward spiral of drug abuse and other criminality.

At that point, he was into wearing baggy pants and graffiti tagging, relatively small-time stuff compared to what he would venture into next. His friend prodded him, "Come on, Ricky. Let's smoke some pot." He tried it, and he liked it. He also enjoyed snorting the lines of cocaine occasionally offered him.

These older boys were actually young men, ages 18 to 22, who were already hooked on cocaine and heroin. They needed someone like Ricky and his friend to do dirty work for them, such as breaking into cars to steal radios and burglarize homes for TVs, VCRs, camcorders, and other valuables.

The older addicts would market the stolen goods for cash, supply the young kids with drugs, and include them in their drug parties. They became Ricky's mentors and male role models, which he lacked at home. Ricky, his two younger brothers, and his younger sister were the products of different fathers, none of whom married their mother or lived with the family.

The drugs and crime lifestyle appealed to Ricky. He estimates that he has burglarized 15 homes and 40 cars. He recalls, "I got caught up in it. It was fun." The fun stopped, however, when he was caught breaking into a car at age 13 and spent his first days in juvenile hall.

Some of Ricky's addict buddies were also gang members, and it was not long before Ricky was "jumped in" to a gang. Soon he was involved in drive-by shootings against rival gang members. In a 2-year period, four of his "homeboys," ranging in age from 13 to 25, fell victim to violent deaths. One was by suicide and the three others were from gang-related gunfire.

Drugs also contributed to Ricky's difficulties in school. He was in seventh grade for only 3 months before he was kicked out for giving another student strong prescription pills he had gotten from a friend. Ricky has not been back to a regular school since then, bouncing between alternative schools and juvenile institutions. He was interviewed for this book from the juvenile institution in which he was serving his second 6-month commitment before his 16th birthday. He has been assigned to a special drug and alcohol therapeutic program to help him overcome his cocaine and heroin addictions.

According to a recent presentation by the deputy director of the California Department of Corrections, 80% of the 160,000 current inmates in California's adult prison system were committed on drug-related charges. They were under the influence of drugs or alcohol at the time they committed crimes.[1] Early drug and alcohol use have also been consistently identified as one of the multiple correlates of serious, violent juvenile offending.[2]

Ultimately, tougher laws or longer periods of confinement will do little to control the "Rickys" of this world. Such external forces seldom produce the desired internal changes. Soon after release, multiple-problem youth such as Ricky merely become better at finding ways to continue doing what they have always done without getting caught.

To make lasting changes, they must be taught new values and skills in a supportive, caring environment. They must also be assisted in breaking their emotional attachment to drugs and alcohol. Absent this, Ricky and too many 8% youth like him will continue to be the majority of residents of our nation's burgeoning jail and prison populations.

Notes

1.   Statistics were provided as part of a roundtable discussion with the heads of the State Criminal Justice Agencies, Association for Criminal Justice Research (California), 49th semi-annual meeting, April 1999, Sacramento, CA.

2.   Huizinga, D., & Jakob-Chien, C. (1998). The contemporaneous co-occurrence of serious violent offending and other problem behavior. In R. Loeber & D. P. Farrington (Eds.), <u>Serious, violent juvenile offenders: Risk factors and successful interventions</u>, (pp. 47-67). Thousand Oaks, CA: Sage.

6

Gangs, Runaways, and Thieves
Definitely the Wrong Crowd

In Chapter 1, we discussed the "predelinquency" problem indicators associated with 8% youth, including associating with gang members, repeatedly running away from home, and a pattern of stealing. We also noted that each of these factors further isolates a young person from positive adults and peers and builds a closer association with "the wrong crowd." In this chapter, we further examine the impact of membership in this not-so-exclusive group and, particularly, the relationship between chronic juvenile offending and juvenile gangs.

Does anyone doubt the notion that there is a group in society labeled "the wrong crowd?" How often have you heard that so-and-so got in trouble because of hanging around with "them"? Certainly, no one sets out to join, but somehow these 8% kids find each other, by design or out of desperation – more likely the latter.

A young gang member we will call Jaime fits this profile. His goal in life is to fit in with his neighborhood gang and not to hit a Little League home run or get an "A" in math. Jaime's parents have little control over him or any of his six brothers and sisters, which include an older brother currently locked up for armed robbery. Before even finishing elementary school, Jaime and his friends broke into a car to steal the stereo. This escapade caused Jaime to see juvenile hall for the first time. At age 11, shortly after his release, Jaime and his friends attempted the same crime again, again failed, and spent more time in custody.

Jaime and his friends are indifferent toward school, if not outright hostile. Jaime neglects his homework and often skips school. When he does go to school, he tends to get into trouble. As a result, he was kicked out of two different junior high schools for fighting and stealing and had to repeat the seventh grade.

For recreation, Jaime's gang smokes marijuana and uses methamphetamines. He has been involved in many shoot-outs with rival gang members from other neighborhoods and watched a fellow "homeboy" die in one shooting. He carries a blackjack, he says, "for protection." By age 14, Jaime had served time in custody on three separate occasions.

Jaime's lack of concern for the law and the rights of others goes well beyond immaturity. Despite his poor showing in school, he is not stupid. Like other 8% youth, he knows he needs to comply with rules and norms in certain situations. He lacks the prosocial values and internal controls, however, that most people have and that society needs to prevent chaos, anarchy, and rampant crime. Jaime is marching to the beat of a different drummer. His gang is setting the tempo, and its members have little inter-est in the welfare of others.

Gang membership has been shown to be related to higher levels of delinquent and criminal behavior, particularly serious and violent offend-ing.[1-3] At the time the 8% Problem studies were completed, gang associa-tion was also found to be an important 8% risk factor. Among the 8% risk factors identified, however, gang association did not appear to be as strong an individual predictor as were some of the other factors. This is believed to be related to the lower overall quality of the data available on gang members and associates for the 1987 offender study group.

In 1997, with much improved information on gangs, our research staff reexamined the rate at which new crimes were committed by first-time wards of the juvenile court. This analysis used data for a sample of youth termi-nating from probation supervision in 1996 and controlled for initial risk classification, age, and the gang status of minors as new probationers. As shown in Table 6.1, the "gang" risk factor resulted in new crime rates nearly double or more than double the rate for youths not belonging to a gang.

It appears that as law enforcement agencies gather better information on gangs and share that information, there is even stronger evidence that gang members are more likely to become serious repeat offenders.[4-7] Additional data aimed at measuring the relative strength of each 8% risk factor is being gathered as part of the current 8% Early Intervention Pro-gram evaluation.

Orange County has developed a comprehensive approach to combat-ing the threat to public safety posed by juvenile gangs. The TARGET program[8] goes far beyond sharing a common computer database. It ex-tends into the streets, where police officers and sheriff deputies ride side by side in teams with district attorney investigators and probation officers in gang-infested neighborhoods during high-crime times, such as Friday and Saturday nights.

The program evaluation results indicate that such intensive and coop-erative gang violence suppression efforts succeed in taking gang leaders and troublemakers "off the street."[9] In addition, the the number of deaths attributed to gang violence has decreased sharply countywide in recent years. This finding is believed to be attributable, at least in part, to TAR-GET program efforts.

TABLE 6.1   Orange County Probation Department
                       1996 Juvenile Supervision Case Terminations (N = 1,665)

Initial Supervision Classification	% of Total Cases	Age at Initial Classification[a]	New Law Violation Rate (%)
Low	10	16 and older	8
	2	15 and younger	6
		If gang is a risk factor	
		16 and older	14 (vs. 7)
		15 and younger	na
Medium	41	16 and older	17
	32	15 and younger	26
		If gang is a risk factor	
		16 and older	27 (vs. 14)
		15 and younger	50 (vs. 19)
High	49	16 and older	33
	66	15 and younger	48
		If gang is a risk factor	
		16 and older	44 (vs. 25)
		15 and younger	56 (vs. 39)

SOURCE: Juvenile Profile Outcome Database – 1996 Terminated Cases (first-time wards), Orange County Probation Department (August 14, 1997).

a. The total number in each age group: 16 and older, 988 cases; 15 and younger, 677 cases.

Orange County is proud of the documented success and popularity of its gang violence suppression efforts. The financial and community support for expanded TARGET activities is proof.

Unless we want to place a police officer on every street corner, however, we will not win the battle against gangs for our 8% potential youth. We need to intervene early in the lives of these young people. They need stability in their lives so that they can build the skills and values that will enable them to become law-abiding and contributing members of our communities as young adults.

Notes

1.   Cohen, B. (1969) The delinquency of gangs and spontaneous groups. In T. Sellin and M. D. Wolfgang (Eds.), Delinquency: Selected studies. New York: John Wiley.

2.   Klein, M. W., Gordon, M. A. & Maxson, C. L. (1986). The impact of police investigation on police-reported rates of gang and non-gang homicides. Criminology, 24, 489-512.

3.   Klein, M. W. , Gordon, M. A. & Maxson, C. L. (1989). Street gang violence. In N. A. Weiner &, M. E. Wolfgang (Eds.), Violent crime, violent criminals. Newbury Park, CA: Sage.

4.   Fagan, J. (1990). Social processes of delinquency and drug use among urban gangs. In C. R. Huff (Ed.), Gangs in America. Newbury Park, CA: Sage.

5.   Thornberry, T. F. (1996). The contribution of gang members to the volume of delinquency. Fact sheet prepared for the U.S. Department of Justice, Office of Juvenile Justice and Delinquency Prevention, Washington DC.

6.   Battin, S., Hill, K. G., Hawkins, J. P., Catalano, R. F. & Abbott, R. (1996). Testing gang membership and association with anti-social peers as independent predictors of social behavior. Paper presented at the annual meeting of the American Society of Criminology, Chicago.

7.   Huizinga, D. (1997). Gangs and the volume of crime. Paper presented at the annual meeting of the Western Society of Criminology, Honolulu, HI.

8.   TARGET (Tri-Agency Gang Enforcement Team) is a collaborative model developed in association with local city police agencies, the Orange County Probation Department, and the Orange County District Attorney's Office. The police agencies include the Orange County Sheriff's Department and police departments in the cities of Fullerton, Anaheim, La Habra, Garden Grove, Westminster, Santa Ana, Costa Mesa, and Orange.

9.   Capizzi, M., Cook, J. I. and Schumacher, M. (Fall 1995). The TARGET model: A new approach to the prosecution of gang cases. The Prosecutor, 18-21.

Part II

Toward an 8% Solution

7

Laying the Groundwork
Devising an Intervention Strategy

There will never be enough money, people, or programs to solve all the problems faced by each youth in our society. In the fight against juvenile crime, we must focus our efforts on the group with the greatest potential to burden and victimize society and the ones most likely to fail in life. This group cries out for our attention.

On completing the 8% studies described previously, the Orange County Probation Department took on the task of developing a program that could help solve our 8% Problem. We could not idly sit and watch new waves of 8% youth enter the juvenile justice system each year, developing nearly unchecked into chronic juvenile offenders and, often, into adult criminals. Seeking an 8% Problem solution has become even more crucial because juvenile crime is expected to increase significantly during the next decade.

There will soon be more juveniles in the 10- to 17-year-old age group than there were in the past 20 years. This population is increasing at a rate of approximately 2% per year throughout the United States, and in some parts of California, including Orange County, it is increasing by as much as 2.5% to 3% per year. The period between 2000 and 2005 will see the greatest growth in the 13- to 15-year-old age group, the primary source of our 8% Problem. We are currently in what might be viewed as the "calm before the storm" and, when it comes, we want to be better prepared.

Building more juvenile halls and jails throughout the United States cannot be our only response. Keeping juveniles and adults behind bars and barbed-wire fences is not cheap. Inmates must be fed, clothed, have their medical needs met, escorted to court hearings, and kept under tight security. Institutional costs for jails and juvenile detention in Orange County can be as high as $120 per day, depending on the institution and how costs are calculated. This is comparable to or higher than what it costs to stay one night in a motel or hotel. Multiply this amount by hundreds of inmates, spending weeks, months or years in confinement, and the cost is staggering.

From 6 years of tracking during our 8% Problem studies, we learned that each chronic juvenile offender costs Orange County taxpayers $44,000 based solely on the average costs of incarceration. Each year, at least 500 new 8% potential youth enter the juvenile justice system in Orange County, and with them a new burden of $22 million falls to taxpayers for their future lockup costs alone.[1]

During the 6 years from their first crime resulting in an arrest and a police request for prosecution, these 8% kids also averaged eight such referrals (six as juveniles and two as adults) and served an average of 19.6 months locked up in custody.

Not included in the $44,000 per minor estimate are the expenses of the police in making the arrest, the youth's prosecution or defense attorney, court operations, probation intake, investigation, supervision, or any other court-ordered actions. One can only guess the real costs in dollars, pain, and suffering caused by each new group of these 8% kids. In a recent article in the <u>Journal of Quantitative Criminology</u>, however, M. A. Cohen estimates that the monetary value of saving a high-risk youth is from $1.7 to $2.3 million.[2]

We believe the real solution to the 8% Problem lies in addressing the social underpinnings of crime and chronic offending as identified in our research. It is to this end that we have devoted substantial efforts during the past 5 years. At the Orange County Probation Department, we are completely rethinking how we approach juvenile crime. We are putting far more emphasis than in the past on the "front end" of the system — the youthful offenders who have not yet committed serious crimes. Others have joined in to help, and we are making progress.

Sharing Our Progress

To date, our efforts toward an 8% Problem solution comprise the following three phases:

- Program design
- Field testing the program model to identify any critical missing program resources or needs to modify our implementation plan
- Formal program evaluation

We have completed the first two phases. The last phase began in June 1997 and will be completed in June 2001. Therefore, why write this book before the final program evaluation results are in?

We believe this is an important time to share some of what we have learned about intervening in the lives of these very troubled youth and families, both from the research literature and from our own trials and errors. First, there is renewed interest in delinquency prevention and, particularly, risk-focused early intervention strategies. Criminal justice practitioners from throughout the country have inquired about our 8% Early Intervention Program. We think others can benefit from our discoveries and, we hope, avoid our growing pains. In addition, we want to ensure that corrections practitioners have an understanding of what they are venturing into, should they seek to join us in solving the 8% Problem. Although the benefits are great, it is not an easy road. There are many pitfalls and frustrations, some of which can be avoided through wise implementation choices, the provision of critical resources, and "hands-on" management and research support.

Furthermore, some of the elements critical for program success take time to develop. Hence, the sooner a community can begin to build these elements, the sooner it can solve the 8% Problem. For example, the Orange County Probation Department had a potent volunteer force in place. We also needed to build closer ties with schools, city officials, and community-based organizations, however, to gain support for our program and overcome the "not in my backyard" syndrome.

In addition, it takes time to develop the understandings and institute the procedures necessary to properly identify potential 8% offenders. Our department had a huge head start in this area. We developed and have been using risk/needs assessment procedures with all our adult and juvenile supervision cases since 1985, following the model developed by the National Institute of Corrections (NIC).[3] These procedures enable the department to classify cases for high, medium, or low supervision. They validly predict which groups of probationers are most likely to re-offend.

The 8% risk factors have a related but somewhat different intent, which is to identify potential serious, chronic juvenile offenders at the beginning of their criminal careers and target them for more intense early intervention. Thus, as we began to work on the 8% Problem solution, our staff were already familiar with risk assessment concepts and there were procedures already in place to gather much of the needed information beginning at the front end of the system.

The Underlying Framework for Intervention

After completing the 8% Problem studies described in Part I, we received a technical assistance grant from the National Institute of Corrections to develop a theoretical model and plan for an 8% Early Intervention Program. We assembled a program design team from many disciplines because of the multitude of problems presented by potential 8% youth and families. The design team included representatives of the probation department, Anaheim's high school district, and the county agencies providing child and family support services. The probation department proposed a pilot early intervention project in Orange County's heavily urbanized northern region because of its large number of kids at risk of becoming chronic juvenile offenders.

Initially, team members from outside of the probation department functioned as consultants. They were prepared to provide advice to the department on what approaches to take, but still viewed 8% youth and families as the probation department's problem and not theirs. Members of the Criminal Justice Department at Temple University in Philadelphia and staff from the NIC provided technical assistance to the design team. These consultants saw the need for services to be integrated and for sister agencies to work together as true collaborative partners. Although a worthy goal, this transition did not occur easily or overnight.

In March 1994, the program design team began its work. It met frequently during the next 6 months to review the 8% study findings, and to research literature on serious, chronic juvenile offenders, and promising intervention strategies. The team sought to design a program model based on the 8% Problem studies and well-substantiated national research on delinquency and not based on gut feelings, pet projects, or individual whims.

Targeting the Right Kids

The factors identified in the 8% Problem studies for predicting serious, chronic juvenile crime were well supported in the criminal justice research reviewed by the design team. Team members noted that many of the 8% risk factors are closely associated with other high-risk behaviors, such as school dropout, teen pregnancy, serious emotional problems, and family violence, which were all topics of concern for individual team members.

The literature review also identified other factors that can further undermine the efforts of multiproblem teenagers and families to cope with life, including poverty, discrimination, social isolation, family or neighborhood violence, and reduced access to educational, cultural, and job opportunities.[4-12] From this review process, the team reached consensus that the 8% risk factors as described in Part I provide a sound basis for selecting the program's target population.

Family-Focused Intervention

Of critical importance was the research done on treatment programs for high-risk youth for the U.S. Department of Justice.[13] This research concluded that for early intervention to have a significant and long-lasting impact, it must focus on the entire family and not just on a youth's delinquent behavior. As a result, the design team agreed that providing services to strengthen the family and helping parents to be better parents would be an important program element.

The team also expressed a belief that families provide the best opportunity to develop trust, values, and a sense of belonging in young people. Therefore, it was agreed that the program would give priority to keeping families intact whenever possible, using out-of-home placements only as a last resort, and developing strategies to empower families to solve their own problems.

Impacting Antisocial Behavior

The program design team reviewed other intervention strategies linked by sound research to reducing the likelihood of youth becoming serious, chronic juvenile offenders. Included among these were methods to

- equip at-risk youth with the skills to maintain self-esteem and gain access to opportunities;[14, 15] examples included helping kids overcome learning problems, improve their social and communication skills, develop interests and special talents, increase feelings of self-worth, and gain greater acceptance among prosocial peers.

- help young people develop long-range goals and dreams.[16]

- develop a positive personal relationship with at least one parent or, in the absence of one or both parents, at least one caring adult.[17-20]

Related to implementing these ideas, the design team recommended the use of "cognitive-behavioral" methods, which can help both an offender and his or her family members to function better in society. Cognitive-behavioral approaches focus on our automatic reactions to the situations around us and how these reactions are related to our basic attitudes and belief systems. For some kids, it may be quite natural to get into a shoving and shouting match over a snide remark made by a classmate. For others, it would be natural to either ignore the remark or respectfully note that the comment was not appreciated. These are cognitive-behavioral differences that, to some degree, can be taught.

Using this approach, three factors are evaluated: the circumstances in which a behavior occurs, the behavior itself, and the consequences of the behavior for the individual. The goal is to identify alternative, socially acceptable behaviors that allow youth and family members to meet their needs and not get into trouble. To better explain how this approach works, we discuss "John," whose description is a composite of several teenagers currently in the 8% Early Intervention Program.

John is 14 years old and lives with his mother, an older brother, and younger sister in a small, one-bedroom apartment in a low-income area. Gangs and illegal drug activity abound. His mom works two jobs to pay the bills, leaving early in the morning and not returning until after 8 p.m. Since his mother and father divorced, John sees his father only approximately once a month.

John's lifestyle and living conditions invite trouble. Unsupervised after school, he begins to hang out with the local gang and is introduced to drinking, smoking marijuana, and sniffing glue and other inhalants. His interest in school decreases. He skips classes and then whole days of school. As his appetite for drugs and alcohol increases, he needs cash. He joins his friends in selling small amounts of drugs and starts breaking into cars to steal radios and valuables left lying on the seats. When he is caught in one such break-in, he winds up in the juvenile justice system.

John fits the 8% risk profile. His behavior is certainly unacceptable. Given his circumstances, however, it is understandable. He enjoyed the immediate, short-term results of his behavior before getting caught. The company of his new friends filled a void in his life. The "highs" from drug and alcohol abuse were pleasurable for awhile.

Part of the cognitive-behavioral approach for John involved linking him with an uncle who was willing to spend the early afternoons and evenings with him, providing stability and a good role model. The uncle helps John with homework and to prepare the evening meals. They also spend leisure time together, playing basketball and watching television. This new relationship has been key to changing John's circumstances that led to his aberrant behavior, which led to the negative consequences. From his uncle, John is getting the extra supervision and support needed to promote prosocial life choices and competencies.

Similar approaches were developed to address John's other problem behaviors, which include drug and alcohol abuse, gang involvement, and truancy. These approaches included relapse prevention, improving communication skills, tutoring, and developing leisure-time interests. These activities helped to occupy his free time more productively and keep him away from gangs.

Initially, it is necessary to provide frequent tangible rewards for youth and parental attempts to try new behaviors. As skills are practiced and enhanced, praise from others, feelings of self-confidence, and pride in accomplishments reduce the need for more tangible rewards.

Case Management Philosophy and Principles

The design team agreed that deputy probation officers would be the primary case managers with the final say in casework decisions. Representatives from other agencies, however, were concerned about how much input they would have regarding the decisions made in individual cases. Such "turf battles" appear to be natural by-products of collaboratives. Although someone ultimately has to be responsible and in charge, staff from other agencies must see value in the program and feel valued in their supportive roles.

As we discovered, conflicts inevitably occur when specialists from a variety of disciplines view progress and setbacks differently. To illustrate, we discuss a hypothetical case involving "Arturo." His school attendance has improved and he has completed half of his community service requirement, hence Arturo is pleasing his teacher and a family counselor. Arturo's mother, however, reports he is coming home late and associating with older gang members. His probation officer plans to file a probation violation for the second "dirty" drug test this month.

The issue is not so much "who" will decide Arturo's fate but "how." Also, what options are available for him to continue in the program or be removed from it? Are there rewards for good behavior and punishments besides juvenile hall? In Orange County, we created a management oversight committee with members from all the partner agencies to get the program operating and to resolve problems such as those in Arturo's case.

Getting Everyone to Work on the Same Page

Another design challenge was to fit the 8% Early Intervention Program into the missions of the varied agencies. Why would a government or nonprofit agency want to be part of this program if it did fit into the agency's mission or purpose? As the interrelated problems of 8% youth and their families were reviewed and key design elements identified, the team members could see the benefit of undertaking this challenge and its relationship to their respective agency goals.

The probation department's mission is to protect the community by conducting investigations for the court, enforcing court orders, and resocializing offenders. To do so, we seek to balance three essential objectives:[21]

Holding offenders accountable for their actions: This means paying restitution, doing community service, or making amends in some other form, such as fines or charity contributions, as directed by the court.

Building an offender's competence: This is done so probationers have the skills to become successful, contributing members of the community. Academics and job skills are the most obvious competence builders. Many of these young people and their parents, however, also need to collaterally develop social skills, get help to cope with tragedy in their lives, and get treatment to overcome drug addictions or alcoholism.

Ensuring the public's right to a safe community: Probation officers are empowered by law to enforce the orders of the court in supervising adult and juvenile offenders to ensure their compliance with the terms of their probation. If needed, probation officers use their arrest powers to remove offenders from the streets who pose immediate threats to community safety.

Although making the community a safer place was not a primary focus for design team members other than those of the probation department, all were involved with and concerned about building the skills of at-risk youth and families and holding them accountable for the results of their behavior. Therefore, each participating agency could find a "comfort zone" with regard to parts of the overall probation department mission.

Community Service: Who Benefits?

Related to juvenile offender accountability, 8% design team members endorsed the use of meaningful community service projects, particularly those that repay society while building character and empathy for the victims of crime and other hardships. Through these types of projects, teenagers build a sense of self-worth, and others may view them in a more positive light.

For example, the probation department previously developed a program in which teenage offenders incarcerated in a juvenile correctional institution could visit a school for severely physically disabled young children and help them overcome their handicaps. Many young men in the program were considered tough gang members in their home neighborhoods, but in the program they developed compassion for the severely handicapped children in their care. They were assigned as orderlies to help young children confined to elaborate prosthetic devices to exercise their limbs, often in a swimming pool.

The effects on both the receiver and the giver were significant. Becoming friends was just one of the benefits. Some of the young men in the program have gone on to find jobs in a field closely related to their community service work.

The 8% Early Intervention Program Goals

Ultimately, six goals were developed to guide the specific intervention strategies. The following goals are aimed at breaking the escalating pattern of criminal and antisocial behavior with 8% potential youth that often begins before they are teenagers and continues into adulthood:

1. To increase structure, supervision, and support to potential 8% minors and their families and link them with people and support services in the community that promote self-sufficiency and good behavior

2. To make potential 8% youth accountable for their actions while helping them to become sensitive to the impact their actions have on others

3. To ensure that these young people and their parents understand the importance of attending school regularly and to otherwise help them succeed in academics and build the skills they need to become responsible, self-sufficient adults

4. To promote prosocial values, behavior, and relationships by providing (i) opportunities for minors to directly help people and improve conditions in their respective communities; (ii), greater access and exposure to positive adult and juvenile role models; and (iii), positive leisure time activities that complement each minor's interests, skills, and abilities

5. To develop intervention strategies and services that are close to home, tailored to the unique needs of individual families, and seek to empower them to solve their own problems in the future

6. To instill a strong commitment to teamwork by all the partners in the intervention program, including the minor's family and community

Anticipated Program Benefits

The 8% Early Intervention Program was designed to first target improvements in school attendance and performance, in family communication and participation in the lives of youngsters, and in positive peer relationships during the 12 to 18 months of each youth's and his or her family's involvement in the program. By participating in the program, families should be better able to resolve their problems and gain access to the services they need. Youths should reduce their involvement in gangs and drug and alcohol abuse and see less need to run away from home or to steal.

The true measure of success in juvenile crime intervention, however, is reducing crime during the long term, approximately 18 to 24 months after the program has been completed. For those who complete the 8% Early Intervention Program, we expect

- Fewer new law violations
- Fewer court appearances (for new crimes or probation violations)
- Fewer days in custody
- Fewer minors who become adult offenders
- Fewer siblings referred for probation and family crisis intervention

The 8% Early Intervention Program design team spent nearly a year laying the groundwork and plans for the program's implementation. This time of research and planning together has served us well. The key design concepts and broad program goals remain unchanged. Only the manner in which the goals are being addressed has changed. How these changes occurred will be discussed later.

Notes

1.   There are approximately 6,500 new (first-time) referrals to the juvenile justice system in Orange County each year. On the basis of our department recidivism study findings, at least 8% of this group can be expected to have three additional referrals (a total of four) during the 3-year period following their initial referral disposition. These baseline studies (i.e., the tracking of large initial referral cohorts) have been repeated three times for 1985, 1987, and 1989 cohorts with very similar results: 8% to 10% of each cohort became chronic juvenile offenders.

2.   Cohen, M. A. (1998). The monetary value of saving a high-risk youth. Journal of Quantitative Criminology, 14, 5-33.

3.   From 1982 to 1985, the Orange County Probation Department worked with the NIC and the Office of Juvenile Justice and Delinquency Prevention to implement NIC's Model Probation Case Management System through its field operations. As part of this effort, our research staff worked with a variety of consultants to develop and validate our juvenile instrument (see Appendix B). The Orange County Juvenile Risk/Needs Assessment instrument is currently being used in many California counties and other jurisdictions throughout the United States, with appropriate adjustments based on local testing.

4.   Loeber, R., & Stouthamer-Loeber, M. (1986). Family factors as correlates and predictors of juvenile conduct problems and delinquency. In N. Morris and M. Tonry M. (Eds.), Crime and justice: Annual review of research. Chicago: University of Chicago Press.

5.   Wilson, J. Q., & Hernstein, R. (1985). Crime and human nature. New York: Simon & Schuster.

6.   Farrington, D., & Hawkins, D. (1991). Predicting participation, early onset and later persistence in officially recorded offending. Criminal Behavior and Mental Health, 1, 1-33.

7.   Greenwood, P. (1992). Reforming California's approach to delinquent and high-risk youth. In J. Steinberg, D. Lyon, and M. Varana (Eds.), Urban America: Policy choices for Los Angeles and the nation. Santa Monica, CA: RAND.

8.   Huizinga, D., Loeber, R. & Thornberry, T. (1993). Urban delinquency and substance abuse. Washington, DC: U.S. Department of Justice, Office of Juvenile Justice and Delinquency Prevention.

9.   Huizinga, D., Esbensen, F., & Weiher, A. (1991). Are there multiple pathways to delinquency? Journal of Criminal Law and Criminology, 82, 83-118.

10. Wright, K., and Wright, K. (1992). <u>Family life and delinquency and crime: A policymaker's guide to the literature</u>. Washington, DC: U.S. Department of Justice, Office of Juvenile Justice and Delinquency Prevention.

11. Nagin, D., & Farrington, D. (1992). The onset and persistence of offending. <u>Criminology, 30</u>, 501-523.

12. Rutter, M. (1987a). Continuities and discontinuities from infancy. In J. Osotsky, (Ed.), <u>Handbook on infant development</u> (2nd ed.). New York: John Wiley.

13. Kumpfer, K. (1993). <u>Strengthening America's families: Promising parenting strategies for delinquency prevention</u>. Washington, DC: U.S. Department of Justice, Office of Juvenile Justice and Delinquency Prevention.

14. Rutter, M. (1990). <u>Psychosocial resilience and protective mechanisms</u>. (pp. 316-331), New York: American Orthopsychiatric Association.

15. Richardson, G., Neiger, B., Jensen, S., & Kumpfer, K. (1990). The resiliency model. <u>Health Education, 21</u>, 33-39.

16. Rutter, M., & Quinton, D. (1984). Long-term follow-up of women institutionalized in childhood. Factors promoting good functioning in adult life. <u>Journal of Developmental Psychology, 18</u>, 225-234.

17. Werner, E. (1986). Resilient offspring of alcoholics: A longitudinal study from birth to age 18. <u>Journal of Studies of Alcoholism, 47</u>, 34-40.

18. McCord, J. (1991). Family relationships, juvenile delinquency and adult criminality. <u>Criminology, 29</u>(3), 557-580.

19. Mulvey, E., & LaRosa, J., Jr., (1986). Delinquency cessation and adolescent development: Preliminary data." <u>American Journal of Orthopsychiatry, 56</u>(2), 212-224.

20. Rutter, M. (1987b). Early sources of security and competence. In J. S. Bruner & A. Garten (Eds.), <u>Human growth and development</u>. London: Oxford University Press.

21. In 1989, Orange County adopted the "Balanced Approach" case management system originally developed by D. Maloney, D. Romig, and T. Armstrong [(1988). Juvenile probation: The balanced approach. <u>Juvenile and Family Court Journal, 39</u>, - (3)].

8

From the Ivory Tower to the Street

Field Testing the Program Model

Although there is now evidence that some approaches to deterring juvenile crime work better than others,[1,2] in the fall of 1994 we were entering into uncharted waters by seeking to combine many varied components into a single intervention program. In addition, we were unwilling to commit an extensive amount of funding and staff effort, and ask others in our collaborative to do the same, without evidence that this concept would work.

Before setting up a complete program with an experimental research design involving random assignment, a field test of the pilot program was planned to "shake down" how cases were selected and what combination of services should be attempted. The field test was targeted to begin in October 1994, to involve up to 40 potential 8% youth and families, and to last 6 to 9 months.

Probation researchers structured the field test so that preliminary program results could be compared to a similar sample of cases from the 1987 8% Problem studies. Our intent was to determine if this effort was worth it. If, after several months, the field test showed no improvement over the way we did business beforehand, we agreed to bring the project to a halt.

In addition to testing the overall effectiveness of the broad program concepts discussed in Chapter 7, the field test was also designed to evaluate

1. Our ability to streamline our intake services so that potential 8% youth could be more quickly identified and begin receiving services

2. The ability of the collaborative to work together as a team to resolve problems in the lives of potential 8% youth and their families

3. Our ability to mobilize volunteers and community-based youth-serving organizations to work more intensively with these high-risk teenagers and their families than they had in the past

4. What, if any, program components should be altered, expanded, or added before the formal program evaluation effort was begun

Refining the Target Population

Prior to field test initiation, the target population selection criteria were refined to include juvenile offenders age 15½ and younger with at least three of the four 8% risk factors discussed in Part I. We also limited case selection to the cities of Anaheim and neighboring Buena Park in north Orange County because of the relatively large number of young people fitting our risk profile from these areas.

The probation department currently diverts many of the more than 1,000 cases it receives each month as referrals for potential criminal prosecution into an informal probation supervision program, which includes a restitution plan and community service hours for the minor to perform. Many other cases are dismissed by the probation department, the district attorney's office, or juvenile court as not serious enough to cause the juvenile to come before the court and be placed on formal probation supervision. Others are dismissed for a lack of sufficient evidence to "make" the case.

To place all cases meeting the 8% risk profile initially referred to the probation department in a highly intensive intervention program would greatly expand the pool of young people currently served by the probation department and the juvenile court, especially if these cases were not destined for formal probation supervision. Hence, the program design team agreed to limit those served by the pilot program to juvenile offenders who had been declared wards of the juvenile court and placed on probation supervision for the first time. If we could succeed with this challenging group of 8% potential kids, we believed we could succeed with any of them.

The Best Laid Plans Gone Bankrupt

As the pilot program was being developed in 1994, the probation department assigned a supervisor and five deputy probation officers to participate. Four of the officers were to carry significantly reduced case loads of 10 to 15 families each, whereas the fifth officer was intended to assist the other four in linking families to volunteers, mentors, and appropriate community resources. The fifth officer would also help develop specialized programming such as weekend retreats for 8% program youth and training for staff in areas such as trauma and conflict resolution.

Our collaborative partners had committed to providing a social worker to assist in evaluating cases, mental health diagnostic services for up to

10 cases, and a school district representative to support the program. The school district also provided a site for weekly staff meetings to evaluate cases, and the probation department earmarked $100,000 of its annual budget to develop a central program headquarters and eventual "one-stop shop" for delivering program services.

In October 1994, the multidisciplinary team was in place, the pilot program was under way, and the field testing was ready to begin. By design, new cases would build slowly at first to permit more time for program development and team building with the program partners. Fewer than 10 cases had worked their way through the initial case staffing process when disaster struck in December 1994.

Like the beginning of World War II in December 1941 sticks to our nation's collective memory, so too is December 6, 1994, remembered as a calamity for Orange County Californians. After years of excellent returns on its money, Orange County government's treasury plummeted dramatically when exotic investments lost much of their value during a year of increasing interest rates. Also, because Orange County served as the investor for approximately 200 additional governmental agencies in Orange County (school districts, water districts, cities, etc.), the loss was compounded. Orange County declared bankruptcy, the largest municipal bankruptcy in U.S. history.[3] Before the pool's investment portfolio could be stabilized, the county investment pool had lost $1.7 billion.

The Orange County Probation Department, like all the agencies affected by the bankruptcy, had to make dramatic cutbacks. Our $68 million budget was almost overnight pared by $9.3 million. A decision had to be made whether to continue with the field test of the model program or wait until some future time, likely years in the future. It became clear that to proceed with the model test, the probation department would basically be on its own. Facing the same budget crisis, the other County of Orange agencies could no longer hire staff to provide direct services. In addition, the probation department had to give up the $100,000 earmarked for opening a central site for the program.

The field test, however, did proceed. We decided to keep the program going even though many other probation services had to be cut. This meant that the probation officers in this program would work with much reduced caseloads compared to those of other probation officers. We lowered the usual caseloads of 70 to 100 cases per officer to 15 youths and their families. Our county government partners at the time, those agencies providing social welfare and health care services, could not afford to dedicate staff to the project in a true collaborative effort. They did, however, have staff members attend weekly meetings with our officers to review individual cases and provide advice as best they could.

At this point, however, there was no central program headquarters to provide a school and array of other services. Although the 8% Early Intervention Program was not being implemented precisely as envisioned, the original goals of the field test could still be addressed. There were also the following encouraging developments:

- The department's newly formed support group, the Probation Community Action Association,[4] put $10,000 into a discretionary fund to meet critical needs of potential 8% youth and families and encouraged the Orange County Board of Supervisors to "keep the program alive."

- Our local chapter of the American Academy of Pediatrics agreed to provide diagnostic services for up to 40 field test families to document critical mental health and health care needs, bolstered by a $10,000 planning grant from their parent agency.

- Probation volunteers rallied to provide more of their available time to work with 8% kids and families, easing the workload demands on probation department staff.

- All five members of the Orange County Board of Supervisors endorsed the probation department's request to proceed with the pilot 8% Early Intervention Program, even as the department struggled to provide basic services.

Essentially, we field tested what could best be described as a family-focused intensive probation supervision program, with a "collaborative twist," as opposed to the full collaborative effort envisioned in a central program site. Even with the limitations, the field test of the 8% Early Intervention Program design was an important learning experience and gave us the initial positive results that encouraged us to press on. It also helped us to refine our internal case selection process and the way we would eventually deliver services.

What was not expected was that this pilot field test would continue for approximately 2 years and cause the 8% Early Intervention Program to become identified as one of the most promising efforts under way in the United States to address the problem of serious, repeat juvenile offending.

Notes

1.   Lipsey, M. W. (1995). What do we learn from 400 research studies on the effectiveness of treatment with juvenile delinquents? In J. McGuire, J. (Ed.), <u>What works? Reducing re-offending</u> (pp. 63-78). New York: John Wiley.

2.   Lipsey, M. W. and Wilson, D. B. (1998). Effective interventions with serious juvenile offenders: A synthesis of research. In R. Loeber & D.P. Farrington (Eds.), <u>Serious and violent juvenile offenders: Risk factors and successful interventions</u> (pp. 313-345). Thousand Oaks, CA: Sage.

3.   The County of Orange officially emerged from its bankruptcy on June 12, 1996.

4.   The Probation Community Action Association was established in 1993 as a private, nonprofit public benefit organization. It is dedicated to supporting the Orange County Probation Department in its efforts to curb juvenile and adult crime. The association assists the probation department by developing special projects that the department cannot develop on its own.

9

All's Well That Ends Well
The Field Test Results

The 8% Early Intervention Program field test officially began in October 1994 and ended in August 1996. During this period, 120 kids and their families received 8% Early Intervention Program services. This was about three times the number originally planned.

Getting New Cases on Board Quickly

One key objective of the field test was to streamline the process used to select and evaluate potential 8% cases. Prior to the initiation of the field test, the average time for probation officers to make their initial contact with new probationers and families was 4 to 6 weeks from the day that the minor officially became a ward of the juvenile court. It could then take an additional 30 to 45 days for field supervision officers to gather the information needed to assess youth and family risk factors and identify critical intervention needs.

By this time, many of the 8% potential kids had already committed new crimes. Hence, they received neither services nor consequences in a timely fashion and were in trouble again. The connection between the crime and the punishment was largely lost. Valuable time in which program services could be started was also lost.

To remedy this problem, potential 8% cases were "flagged" before the final court disposition hearing but without trying to influence the court's decision in the case. Collaborative partners agreed to speed their efforts at information gathering. The school representative tracked down attendance and academic performance information. A social worker checked for court cases involving child abuse or neglect, which would indicate problems in the home. A mental health worker gathered relevant behavioral and medical information.

In the meantime, probation staff conducted criminal record checks and initial interviews with the youths and families. The families were contacted to schedule the initial interview within 2 days of the court's decision. This early contact, which is the first office visit with the minor and parents, is important to answer any immediate questions that parents have regarding their child's probation, to begin to build good relationships, and to explain the court's expectations.

After data gathering and the initial interview, cases not meeting the program's selection criteria were transferred to a regular probation supervision caseload. For those kids matching the 8% risk profile, a home visit followed. The goal of the initial home visit was to identify any pressing problems requiring immediate action. For example, a parent or other person living at home might be physically or emotionally abusing a child and steps must be taken immediately to protect the child.

The net result of the program's efforts was to reduce the time for a youth to enter the program and begin to receive services to just 7 to 10 days after court. This was a significant achievement that we have continued to build on as the intervention program has matured and expanded.

Initial Assessment and Intervention Strategies

Before beginning the field test phase, we sought help from the National Council on Crime and Delinquency, a nationally known consulting firm. They were asked to suggest an assessment form and process with a proven track record for evaluating the relative risk of families for potential child abuse and neglect.

The assessment form they recommended for our use is similar to the Juvenile Risk/Needs Assessment forms we have used since 1983.[1] Officers found this new tool to be very useful, and it has been incorporated into the ongoing initial case assessment process.

An important lesson learned relative to this process was to pay more attention to input from the teenager and family members. Despite their many needs, we must be careful not to develop intervention plans "behind their backs." This puts families on the defensive. They need to be asked what they think is needed in their lives, what goals they have, and what they believe is hindering them from achieving these goals. This helps to develop program "buy-in" so that the family and youth will want to work with our team and be part of the solution. These youth and families need to hear more about their family's strengths and reasons for hope rather than their weaknesses. They already know plenty about those!

During the field test phase, we began to learn how to build on family strengths. For example, kids have entered the program who were at or very near the grade level at which they were supposed to be, despite problems in other areas of their lives. Aided to advance further in school, these kids and their families were motivated to work and make progress in other areas.

We also learned, however, that with the multitude of problems in these homes, no one person can solve them all. Caseworkers get overwhelmed. It is like the mallet game that young children play in arcades: immediately after one knob is struck down, another knob pops up in a different place. With these multiple-problem families, we must target and celebrate small steps in the right direction, expecting that for every two or three positive steps forward, there may be one or two steps back. We can still rejoice in a "net gain."

Experimenting With Community Involvement

Our program design consultants recommended that we pull together broad community participation in developing the 8% Early Intervention Program. During the field test phase, we learned how important this factor would be, especially given the restrictions following the bankruptcy on our own department's budget and those of our sister county agencies. In fact, the willingness of the community to come to our aid was one of the bright spots of the field test effort.

The probation department already had a volunteer contingency with 20 years of experience. These Volunteers in Probation typically number approximately 500 and primarily assist as recreation leaders, Bible study leaders, and visitors for kids who do not get any in the probation department's juvenile institutions. Early in 1993, the department established Volunteer Probation Officers (VPOs), similar in concept to reserve officers in police agencies. VPOs must pass a rigid background test and receive 44 hours of classroom training and 26 hours of on-the-job training, so that they can function more like a regular probation officer. Typically, there are 40 to 70 VPOs assisting our officers in the field at any given time.

Volunteers have been a tremendous asset to the 8% program, particularly during the field test phase. In one fatherless home, the mother worked nights and suffered from psychological problems. The 8% program son was left largely to himself, and his younger brother and sister fell behind in their schoolwork. One volunteer visited the home frequently, whereas another, a college student, met the younger kids at their elementary school for after-school tutoring.

Another dedicated volunteer would drive 40 miles one way from her suburban home twice a week to work with our 8% program families. She was among approximately two dozen volunteers who worked as counselors and presenters at an intense 3-day mountain retreat with 8% and other at-risk youth. Our volunteers build strong relationships with probation youth and families and have been excellent role models. In addition, they provide an extra pair of hands, eyes, ears, and feet to overworked probation staff.

In the fall of 1993, the department was fortunate to bring together businessmen and community leaders from throughout Orange County to form a nonprofit support group called the Probation Community Action Association (PCAA). The PCAA focuses on raising funds for special projects rather than volunteering time to work with individual probationers.

As mentioned in Chapter 8, this group established a discretionary fund which probation officers use to make purchases, helping individual 8% youth and their families in times of crisis or to boost morale. For example, funds were used to buy a dress for a girl for her junior high school graduation, to pay an electric bill to keep the lights on in a family's apartment, to enter a young man into Little League baseball, and to buy clothes for a parent to wear on a job interview.

In one case, a business helped a family of nine move out of an obviously crowded motel room into a three-bedroom apartment. The company provided $1,200 for the apartment's required first and last month's rent and security deposit, with a requirement that $600 be paid back over time. In another instance, an automobile dealer repaired the family car for an indigent household run by a single, out-of-work grandmother.

Although we have to guard against building dependency through repeated financial bailouts, such compassion and well-timed assistance can provide 8% program families the opportunity to achieve order in their households and move beyond temporary crises. For an immature boy or girl, fulfilling a dream of attending a major sports event with dad or getting a professional haircut may provide major motivation to "hang in" and keep working on new behaviors.

After the nonprofit support group secured a Pacific Mutual Foundation grant for an eight-passenger van, we were better able to transport youth and their families to important intervention services and organized special activities as "rewards" for achieving major case goals. Through the PCAA discretionary fund, specialized services such as staff training and anger management counseling for youth were purchased.

Probation staff and volunteers learned how to organize parent education classes and conduct the annual weekend retreats for youth, aided by an inner-city Catholic organization that has developed sound program models for gang youth and their families. This Los Angeles-based program donated many hours of staff and volunteer time to assist us in adapting their models to the unique needs of our target population.

There are many more examples of contributions from Orange County citizens and volunteer organizations to the 8% program's early operations. This outside support was crucial in keeping the program alive during the 2-year field test period while Orange County government worked its way out of bankruptcy. The point is that there are many more resources in our communities than most people think. The trick is to mobilize them for a particular program's benefit.

One nonprofit group that was particularly helpful in this phase of the program was the American Academy of Pediatrics (AAP). Our local AAP chapter adopted the 8% Early Intervention Program when, in the wake of the bankruptcy, we had no means to determine the mental health and health care needs of our youth and families. Through a grant from their parent organization and the equivalent of $30,000 in volunteer service hours, they conducted medical screenings of more than 40 field test cases and their siblings. Their findings, plus an analysis of 10 cases by Orange County's Health Care Agency, gave us tremendous additional insight into the families with whom we were working.

Characteristics of the Field Test Families

In assessing the needs of 8% families, we were struck by their many needs for compassionate assistance, the amount of abuse and violence affecting their lives, and the volume of untreated mental and physical ailments.

Although not all 8% families are poor, poverty was a fairly common denominator. According to Orange County Social Services Agency records, 45% of our field test families were receiving some kind of government financial assistance. It was not unusual for a family to be living in a single, cramped motel room with no kitchenette and no play areas for their children.

Child abuse, although not rampant, was common. From our reports and social services records, we learned that in 14% of the families, the potential 8% minors said they suffered physical abuse at home, whereas in 16% of the families their brothers or sisters reported being physically abused. Sexual abuse was reported by five probation youth, and there were also five cases of the minor's brothers or sisters complaining of sexual abuse.

Broken homes are the norm for these families. Very few of our kids live with both their natural father and mother. Recall "Andrew," the young man mentioned in Chapter 3 who harbored bitterness toward his stepfather, the fifth in Andrew's 13 years of life, and "Danny," who awaits his father's return from prison for armed robbery and murder. Tracking the relationships among family members living under the same roof can be confusing. One probation officer noted, "Family trees are more like vines."

The mental and physical health screenings conducted by the AAP found that 35 of the 49 youth screened were deemed to have "significant" mental health problems. Six children were linked to clinical depression and conduct disorders, and another 6 children had a history of suicidal ideation, 2 of whom were declared "acutely suicidal." Only 1 of the 35 children diagnosed with mental health problems was receiving psychotherapy.

We were amazed to find that more than half of these kids (27 of 49) experienced unresolved psychological trauma due to grief from the loss of a family member within the past 2 years. Most of these kids suffering from unresolved grief had symptoms characteristic of post traumatic stress disorder. Seven youths had "definite and obvious learning disorders" hampering their ability to function in school.

Confirming the evidence of abuse in county social services records, the AAP health care exams revealed 15 children of 49 who either were child abuse victims or lived in families in which child abuse or domestic violence had occurred. One family of 11 members had 20 reports filed against it for physical abuse or neglect, and yet the children were still living in the home. The AAP study concluded that 8% youth in general had little or no access to appropriate mental health or medical preventive care and that too many had undiagnosed and untreated conditions. Less than one third had their needed immunizations. One 4-year-old boy even had an untreated broken arm.

Clearly, our officers had their hands full in trying to deal with the myriad problems of these families. These evaluations revealed that these families desperately needed mental health, health care, drug abuse, and social welfare services. Our officers were frustrated that these services were not part of the formal program nor readily available.

Staff Burnout

As the field test progressed, the probation staff unfortunately became increasingly worn down and worn out. They did not want to give up, but it became clear that probation officers could not go the distance with these high-intensity, problematic cases without considerable help. Ironically, we found that these small, intensive caseloads were more draining on staff than the former ones of 70 or even 100. Officers become much closer to the teenagers and their families than they normally would and to some degree share in their pain, suffering, and setbacks.

Although some youth and families made large gains in academics and family life and reduced crime over time, the many setbacks in between began to take their toll. Our officers worked long and unusual hours in the program, adding to stresses in their own personal lives. Special activities were frequently scheduled on nights and weekends to accommodate the work schedules of 8% program families, and crises invariably occur during off-duty hours.

Also added to this mix was the strain of working in the spotlight of the department's highest profile program, which was being followed coast to coast by corrections specialists and had garnered national media attention. Understandably, many of our officers were ready for new assignments after 1 or 2 years of this intensity.

Retooling

The final field test objective was to identify needs to modify or expand program services before beginning the formal evaluation of the 8% Early Intervention Program. Program staff and researchers deemed the following elements as critical to achieving the desired long-term results and for reducing the toll taken on our staff during the field test phase.

1. Acquiring a program site in the target area capable of housing all key program staff, including an on-site school, to better coordinate the delivery of services

2. Expanding the existing assessment, diagnostic, and direct intervention services, particularly in the areas of mental and physical health problems and drug and alcohol abuse

3. Adding intensive in-home family services to improve family functioning and parent involvement in the program

4. Continuing availability of discretionary funds to meet unique needs and better respond to crises in individual families

5. Developing a broader range of individual and group opportunities for community service and victim-offender mediation

6. Developing service contracts with community-based organizations for parent education, life-skills training, comprehensive employment services, and enrichment activities

7. Expanding transportation services to ensure full participation by youth and family members in key program activities

8. Continuing use of citizen volunteers and community resources to enhance the program and provide support for youth and families that can continue when the formal program ends

9. Continuing participation of researchers in the program's development to ensure the program stays on course, to gather statistics for program evaluation, to provide feedback on program successes, and to recommend "mid-course" corrections

10. Continuing support from each agency's top management to maintain healthy collaborations among agencies, to assign appropriate staff, and to ensure that problem-solving procedures are in place and used by all the collaborative partners

The Bottom Line

The primary purpose of the 8% Early Intervention Program field test was to determine how to best address the program goals outlined by the multidisciplinary design team, to shake down various program processes, and to determine if the pilot project had enough merit to continue.

By August 1996, of the 120 youth and families served, 67 had completed 12 months in the program. Table 9.1 presents case outcomes for these 67 youth compared with those of 42 cases from the 1987 chronic offender subsample meeting the program selection criteria from the original 8% Problem study.

Table 9.1   Comparison of Field Test Cases With 8% Study Time Frame[a]

Group	Percentage With Subsequent Petitions Filed	Probation Violations Only	New Law Violations	Percentage With Subsequent Commitment
Original 8% study group (1987;) (N = 42)	93	21	72	86
8% Field test group (1994-1996;) (N = 67)	49	6	43	43

a. First-time wards, age 15 or younger, with a multiproblem profile

These field test results, although not conclusive, were very encouraging. For the minors in the pilot program, there were far fewer cases filed with juvenile court for both probation and new criminal violations. The number of youth locked up by the juvenile court decreased by half. Although there was much developmental work left to do, we were off to a promising start.

Note

1.   Children's Research Center, National Council on Crime and Delinquency. The Urban Caucus Decision-making Model, (1994). Madison, WI.

10

A Case Study
A Lesson From the Real World

The greatest concern of those who participated in the pilot program was that these positive early results would be short-lived. They feared that once probation officers and volunteers were no longer involved daily in the lives of these families, they would slip back into their old ways and the teenagers would continue on a path leading to crime. Were kids and families temporarily propped up, or were they developing the coping skills to deal with the challenges of day-to-day life?

The field test experience demonstrated that these kids and families would need substantial time and varied opportunities to practice the new skills and behaviors they had begun to learn. To demonstrate the highs and lows that can be expected over the long term, we interject the story of a young woman who was part of the field test study and under probation supervision for 4 years.

Anita's Story

The case of "Anita" illustrates the challenges of working with the most difficult cases in the juvenile system and humanizes our story of program development. It also shows that successes are often tempered, and what may appear as defeats can have silver linings.

Anita would sneak out of elementary school at age 9 to hang out with older gang girls, and she smoked her first marijuana cigarette that year. By age 12, while still a sixth grader, she was fully swept into a world of drug parties and gangs. She was using PCP and rock cocaine to get high. Small-time neighborhood drug sellers rewarded her with pieces of rock cocaine for finding customers. She looked and claimed to be older, and she could slip into parties with older teenagers and young adults in rented motel rooms or family homes when parents were away.

Anita's mother seemed ill equipped to properly supervise her, an infant daughter, and Anita's older brother, who was a longtime criminal gang member. Caught up in her own problems, her mother seemed helpless to stop Anita's self-destructive and delinquent lifestyle, despite the signs of trouble. Anita was staying out late and sleeping until 10 a.m. or noon. She would be "sick" or miss the school bus; thus, she was kicked out of junior high school because of her poor attendance. She had crude tattoos put on each wrist. Anita's relationship with her stepfather, who raised her, was always strained.

Anita's quick temper first got her in trouble with the law at age 11. A young woman twice her age had accused Anita of flirting with her boy-friend. Anita now concedes that she was the aggressor in the vicious fight that followed. Before the juvenile justice system could sort out the ele-ments of this incident, however, Anita was in trouble again.

She rode with older gang members in a stolen vehicle to a local shop-ping mall. After shoplifting clothes from a department store, she and her friends were chased through the parking lot. She and one gang member were caught. Anita went on the run to dodge some of her court dates, hoping her criminal charges would fade away. They did not. Police caught her with friends in an apartment drug bust, and Anita got her first ride to juvenile hall. Her combination of offenses and avoiding the law cost her 2 months of incarceration, before her 13th birthday.

Hence, it was no surprise that Anita would spend all but a few months of her teen years on formal probation. For more than 2 of those years, she was part of the 8% Early Intervention Program during its field test phase. Anita's teenage years were even more turbulent. She was the young woman mentioned in Chapter 3 who nearly lost her life in a gang-related shooting. Her boyfriend at that time, seated in the car beside her, was shot through the back and lung. He recovered in 2 weeks; she nearly died and spent months in and out of the hospital.

Anita suffered short-term memory loss as a result of the shooting and was enrolled in a special education class. Pushed heavily by her proba-tion officer, a school counselor, and her special education teacher, Anita finished junior high school – a seemingly minor stepping stone for most people but a major accomplishment in her family.

The 8% program helped to pull her out of the valleys and reach a few hilltops during her teenage years. The department's support group bought her clothes and shoes to wear to her junior high school graduation. For a year, she tested drug free and had no other probation violations or crimi-nal offenses.

At age 15, Anita fell into a relapse. She got back into drugs, failed her drug urinalysis tests, and was ordered to serve 6 weeks in a juvenile insti-tution. At the same time, Anita discovered she was pregnant by her boy-friend. She would drop out of school in her junior year.

This hardly sounds like a success story, especially to readers who live in more affluent neighborhoods and expect their children to complete high school and attend college. We have learned, however, that progress comes in small steps for this very difficult population. Setbacks can be expected.

With her pregnancy, it became even more important for Anita to be drug free. The incarceration was a good beginning, followed by even more intensive drug and alcohol testing. Both Anita and her mother agreed to attend parenting classes, and Anita began attending a special school for teenage mothers. She says that the responsibilities of being a parent forced her to mature quickly.

The department's support group paid to have her tattoos removed, which she says was critical in gaining self-esteem and putting her gang ties behind her. The tattoo laser removal treatments cost hundreds of dollars, and she would not have undertaken them without financial aid. Three years later, Anita in fact has turned a corner and is making every effort to live crime and drug free and every effort to raise her 2½-year-old child responsibly.

When Anita partied with her gang friends, she had a "live for today" attitude common among her peers. Now she plans ahead. Her efforts to attend school are complicated by the need to care for her child. As of this writing, however, she has taken special classes to be a dental assistant and is in an internship program for that field. She hopes that someday she can complete her high school education and attend a community college.

In a letter to the probation department's support group, Anita described the importance of having her tattoos removed: "Thank you all for your help in changing my life. Now I don't have to worry about people looking down on me because of my tattoos. I will always remember you people as part of my new world, a world without violence, gangs, drugs."

Although there is no crystal ball to see what her future would have been like without an intensive intervention program early in her teen life, Anita's story demonstrates that lives can be changed for the better before it is too late.

11

The 8% Solution
– Orange County Style

True Collaboration and a One-Stop Shop

By August 1996, we had the experience of the field test under our belts, and the effects of the county bankruptcy had largely ebbed. The concept of early intervention based on our 8% Problem studies and field test findings was also drawing significant interest from many legislators in Sacramento, California's state capitol. We were able to convince our state senators and assemblymembers that the juvenile justice system could benefit from targeted early intervention aimed at those young people who we could show had the greatest potential to victimize society.

Support From State Government

In 1996, the California Legislature allocated $3.5 million for a 3-year test of the 8% program concepts. This important demonstration project was called the Repeat Offender Prevention Program (ROPP) and initially involved the following counties: Fresno, Humboldt, Los Angeles, Orange, San Diego, San Mateo, and Solano. During the next 2 years, the funding for the ROPP project was increased to more than $10 million, and the original seven county programs were extended through June 2001. In addition, a new pilot project was funded in San Francisco to begin in 1998.

The Orange County Probation Department was asked to provide technical assistance to the other counties, which were starting their programs from "Ground Zero." In a series of 2-day sessions sponsored by the California Board of Corrections, Orange County staff and researchers provided training to sister counties in how to identify the target population, the theoretical basis for the key program design concepts, and the many important lessons learned from their extended field test experiences. We also shared assessment and case planning forms, staff training materials, and written procedures. We included tips on building collaborative relationships and developing new community-based resources.

In Orange County, the state funds enabled us to add the critical program elements outlined at the end of Chapter 9 to create the multidisciplinary, "one-stop shopping" service delivery approach we call the Youth and Family Resource Center (YFRC). Another state-funding opportunity, the Juvenile Crime and Accountability Challenge Grant program, enabled us to simultaneously enhance our "front-end" assessment procedures for all first-time wards.

The limited dollars initially given to the other six ROPP counties, ranging from $400,000 to $625,000 for the first three project years, were not sufficient to match the type and intensity of services that Orange County was planning to provide. We had a 3-year head start on developing collaborative relationships and resource commitments. Nonetheless, as the other county programs gained momentum and as the Legislature added additional money to support these demonstration projects, the other participating counties have been able to operate programs with enough consistency to test the design concepts underlying Orange County's 8% Solution.

The common elements of the ROPPs are delineated in Appendix C. Also presented is the enabling legislation codified as Sections 743 to 749 of the California Welfare and Institutions Code. The remainder of this chapter is devoted to an explanation of the service delivery approach used in Orange County to implement its 8% Solution. We note, however, that in some counties, regardless of resources, it would never be practical to replicate our preferred approach to service delivery. This is because some counties do not have a large enough concentration of 8% potential youth living in one geographic area to make it feasible to operate a Youth and Family Resource Center.

Like our sister counties in the state-funded project, geographic size or demographic makeup will not prevent any county or jurisdiction from implementing the common program elements and key design concepts inherent in the Orange County 8% Solution. Each jurisdiction will simply need to tailor its service delivery and program development to reflect local needs and resources.

The Youth and Family Resource Center Model

In reality, the way we deliver services in Orange County's 8% Early Intervention Program today was not fully implemented until June 1998. In September 1996, prior to the availability of ROPP funding, we leased a 7,500-square-foot office building along a commercial strip in Anaheim. Leasing this building was a joint investment by the probation department and the Orange County Department of Education, which is reimbursed by the state for educating juvenile court wards based on average daily attendance in class. The center staff initially consisted of only probation officers and teachers.

Although state funds became available in January 1997, it took nearly 18 months to assign county staff, develop contracts with new collaborative partners, purchase additional vans, complete the site buildout, and relocate to this new facility large enough to accommodate our new "family." The current 10,000-square-foot facility was designed to complement the operation of a much expanded multidisciplinary team consisting of the following:

- Five deputy probation officers: four case-carrying officers and a case screener, who also functions as a community resource specialist seeking new resources to meet the unique needs of individual youth and families

- Six deputy probation counselors, who transport minors to and from school, coordinate the schedule of all activities at the center, and work with youth and families in a variety of skill-building activities

- A supervising probation officer who acts as the site manager and team facilitator

- A clerk, who serves as the unit typist and office receptionist[1]

- Up to four teachers and teachers' aides with a capacity for teaching up to 68 students in four classrooms[2]

- A mental health team with one service chief (supervisor), a part-time psychiatrist, a full-time clinical psychologist, two therapists (Licensed Clinical Social Workers or Marriage, Family, and Child Counselors), interns, and clerical support staff who service both probation youth and family members

- Two in-home counselors from a private counseling agency who work with up to 10 families at any given time to improve family functioning and provide crisis intervention services as needed

- A county alcohol and drug abuse counselor, who counsels youth and their parents

- A nurse practitioner, who screens 8% potential youth and siblings for health care problems, provides health education,[3] and assists families in finding a "medical home" for preventive medical care

- A supervisor and 3.5 full-time staff from a community-based organization, who provide parent education, teen parenting, and community service programming and also provide cultural, recreational, and social activities for our kids and families

The YFRC staff have "graduated" from cooperative relationships to true collaborative partnerships. They now do more than share files and consult on difficult cases. Our partners have helped us to enhance the 8% Early Intervention Program model by

- Developing risk verification criteria and procedures
- Refining our case selection process and developing standard case assessment tools[4]
- Tailoring case plans to meet the unique needs and strengths of each youth and family

All partners work on each case, bringing their particular expertise to the table. The weekly staffings have taken on a new dimension. Everyone involved knows each youth and family well. Each views problems from a different vantage point not only because of their unique background training and experience but also because of the different and varied opportunities each has to interact with kids and family members each week. This frequency of contact with many program staff members facilitates quicker identification of individual interests and strengths, thus increasing the likelihood of youth and family "buy-in" to center programs. The combined expertise and knowledge of the multidisciplinary team regarding case dynamics have also resulted in a more rapid and appropriate response to emerging problems.

In one of the more dramatic cases, a youth who had been in the program for more than 1 year and was doing well in school suddenly became sullen, uncooperative, and disinterested. Was there a problem in school? Was the minor having difficulty with another student in class or with a staff member? Were there difficulties at home or with his girlfriend? Was he drinking again? Instead of this young man's internal torment being overlooked and lost in a much larger caseload, several of the collaborating partners recognized the warning signs and set out immediately to get answers. They discovered that the depression suffered by the young man's mother had gotten worse, and that she had attempted suicide. Both the mother and the young man received immediate counseling and intervention to stabilize the home environment.

Life at the Youth and Family Resource Center

We now describe a typical day at the YFRC. The program has been implemented as we originally envisioned it, with its full complement of collaborative partners working side by side on a daily basis.

The program minors are picked up for school by 7:30 a.m. on weekdays and head home between 3:30 and 5 p.m. We use our own deputy probation counselors to conduct on-site supervision and drive the transportation vans. In Orange County, deputy probation counselors are primarily used as the line staff in our juvenile institutions or to supervise weekend work crews of juvenile offenders. We have two 15-passenger vans for the 8% Early Intervention Program, but we also provide bus passes to families and encourage parents to drive on their own to various program activities. To best use our vans and drivers, we sometimes stagger the school start times. A third van will be added in 1999, as the program nears capacity, with up to 60 youth on-site and 15 to 20 youth and families in transitional programming.

On the basis of our current cases, at least two thirds of 8% potential youth have a history of being truant. The YFRC van arriving outside the probationer's door at 7 o'clock each morning or at a nearby pickup point sends a loud and clear message to everyone in the family about school. Education is important, and it is important that each minor take full advantage of the opportunities the YFRC school provides for academic success.

Providing transportation also eliminates most excuses for being absent or late. If a youngster is not ready when the van arrives, the family is called en route to the next stop on a cellular telephone. Unless a reasonable excuse is provided, the van will be back to pick up any "lazy bones" with whatever center staff are needed. If staff believe a youth is feigning illness, he or she may be brought to see the nurse practioner. If the entire family frequently sleeps in on school days, an in-home social worker may team up with the probation officer to work on improving family functioning. This can include arriving before the 7 a.m. van to ensure that everyone is awake and preparing for the day.

The key is for the minor to want to attend school and participate in other center services. This will only happen if the youth has more positive experiences than negative ones each day. Cognitive-behaviorial theory states that to positively reinforce behavior, an individual must experience "good vibes" in a ratio of 4:1 compared to "bad vibes."[5] This poses a real challenge to all center staff.

Orange County and the City of Anaheim have their share of motel families. At one point, five of our north county YFRC kids were living at one motel. One youth took it on himself to be the "waker-upper" for school. Several months ago, one of our vans broke down. Our "motel kids," seeing that the van was late, pooled their change, caught a bus, and made it to the center on time. Obviously, they are experiencing something worthwhile.

Snacks and a light breakfast of fruit and cereal are also available for teenagers who may not have had an adequate breakfast. After breakfast and morning announcements, the kids enter the structured environment of a small school. If home life is chaotic, kids can look forward to safety, structure, and stability in school. Although the YFRC school does not have all the amenities of classes that a typical junior high or high school would have, it does have far fewer distractions and is much less intimidating. Students move along at their own pace and face much less embarrassment. Individual educational plans are developed and coordinated with parents, the school district, and the youth's overall case plan.

Since most of our potential 8% youth are of junior high age, the goal of the school program is to prepare these kids to succeed in a regular comprehensive high school. In the meantime, however, our experience has shown that at least 80% of the teens in the 8% Early Intervention Program initially need the structure and specialized services offered at the center's school, which includes the consistent enforcement of rules that are established to keep order and organize daily activities.

Because no time is needed to shuffle between classes as on a large campus or to change clothes for a physical education class, our on-site school easily packs a full day of academics and classroom instruction into the morning hours before lunch. Sack lunches are served in our multipurpose room.

Afternoon programming can be quite varied, but two staples are recreation and a study hall. By afternoon, the kids need some fresh air, exercise, and a change of scenery. We take the youngsters to the park for a softball game or handball or to a recreation center for basketball and weightlifting. The study hall period provides a quiet time to get homework done, write in a journal, and work on independent study packets to gain extra school credits. Volunteer tutors have helped students who are struggling in reading or with other basic skills. For many of these kids, there is not a quiet place at home to do homework or any encouragement from their parents to complete it. We fill that void.

Approximately two thirds of 8% potential minors abuse drugs, alcohol, or both. Most abuse more than one drug. Our on-site substance abuse counselor begins intervention early. Regardless of their drug abuse history, every youth at a center receives at least 1 hour per week of drug and alcohol abuse education or counseling. Those minors known to have abused illegal drugs or to regularly consume alcohol also receive individual and family counseling. The fact that probation officers can follow up counseling with drug testing, home inspections, and the filing of new charges if necessary puts the authority of the court behind the counselor's efforts. Many youth and family members are responding positively to this collaborative approach.

Mental health team members on site confirmed that more than half of all the kids have mental health problems, including adjustment disorders, conduct, oppositional defiant and disruptive behavior disorders, attention deficit disorder, attention deficit hyperactivity disorder, anxiety disorders, and clinical depression. This should not be surprising, because our assessment information also reveals that nearly half of the 8% kids live in homes involving family violence, and more than 60% involve marital discord. In addition, 20% of the center youth are grieving a recent death in their family, whereas an additional 20% to 25% have diagnosed learning disabilities. It is critical to the success of early intervention efforts that these mental health and learning issues be properly diagnosed and treated.

For the past year, we have used a community-based agency that conducts in-home counseling for the most challenging families in the program. The counselor seeks to meet with 8% youth individually and with family members for 5 or 6 hours per week during a 12-week period, primarily at the family's home. This is a good setting because counselors can obtain a better feel for what home life is truly like by seeing it firsthand. Family members tend to open up and be more honest about their lives at home rather than in an unfamiliar and perhaps intimidating office environment.

Getting parents to genuinely cooperate and participate is another matter. Often, they are naturally defensive and perplexed by the extra attention simply because their teenage son or daughter has committed one or two relatively minor offenses. They may know that they need extra help as parents, but pride can stand in the way of their accepting any outside help or advice.

The first step is building a trusting relationship based on mutual respect. The in-home counselors seek to empower parents to identify and solve their own problems while also learning about resources in their community that can help them. Sometimes building trust and making even small steps toward improved family functioning can take more than the 90 days originally envisioned. For many of these families, 4 or 5 months may be more realistic.

During the past year, the American Academy of Pediatrics (AAP) has again played an important role in the 8% Early Intervention Program. From July to December 1998, the nurse practitioner completed 85 health screening examinations and made 106 diagnoses. Fifteen referrals were made, only half of which saw a physician within 1 week. During the first quarter of 1999, more examinations were performed by the nurse practioner and referrals made to physicians.

The increased percentage of cases that visited a physician, 75% within 1 week of referral, is a dramatic improvement in parental follow-through. It is believed to be attributable to the nurse practioner's and clinical educator's work in family education, particularly on how to access appropriate services.

Another important service provided by the AAP has been the nurse practioner's evaluation of whether a minor is too ill to attend or remain in school. As a result, school absenteeism has been greatly reduced.

On many afternoons and some Saturdays, the focus switches to community service projects. Kids can give back to their communities by planting trees, helping the handicapped, working at a food bank, or cleaning yards for the elderly poor.

A contracted community-based organization searches out and coordinates meaningful projects. This organization also provides victim-offender mediation services, helping victims and offenders to work out problem solutions. For example, teenagers caught pitching rocks from a flood control ditch onto cars driving on a freeway met some of their victims through the mediation service. The rocks sounded like gunshots when they hit cars and broke windows, panicking the motorists. The car window of a family of Canadian tourists was shattered, spraying glass on their baby. Fortunately, no one was hurt. The offending youths and their parents, however, were visibly moved by their encounter with their victims.

Friday afternoons and at least one Saturday per month are reserved for special outings for the kids who were cooperative that week. They are taken to an amusement park, the beach, for a barbecue in the park, or on a field trip to a library, museum, or movie. Special family activities and individual enrichment activities are also coordinated by a community-based organization.

Life skills training is provided on a consistent basis by all team members. Kids are exposed to a range of topics, including planning and preparing nutritious meals, budgeting, balancing a checkbook, problem solving, goal setting, career exploration and counseling, and teen parenting.

Finally, volunteers play an important role at the YFRCs. Tutors help 8% potential kids and their siblings to improve self-esteem through making consistent academic progress. Kids look forward to the special one-on-one attention they receive from a caring adult. Mentors can also be important to both youth and families in making positive changes in their lives through modeling, encouraging, and reinforcing positive behavior. In addition, adult volunteers who share a special skill or take a kid on an outing help to provide the 4:1 ratio of positive to negative reinforcements important to the continued progress of 8% youth.

What Does a Youth and Family Resource Center Cost?

Appendix E delineates the cost of operating a YFRC as described in this chapter in southern California. Obviously, the cost of individual program components will vary by jurisdiction. In some communities, some service components may already be provided through other governmental or public service organizations and, therefore, would not result in new program costs. In Orange County, educational services fall into this category and are not included.

Orange County's YFRC model was designed to serve approximately 60 on-site program youth. During a given year, however, with case turnover and minors transitioning to community schools and support services, the Youth and Family Resource Center is expected to serve approximately 100 discrete youth and families. The total annual cost for each center is approximately $1.4 million. The average program stay is approximately 18 months, including transitional services for youth and families.

Therefore, it costs approximately $14,000 to provide YFRC services to a potential 8% family based on the average current Orange County costs. Several components are eligible for reimbursement, however, and we have not factored in any cost recovery.

Even at full cost, the YFRC compares favorably to incarcaration at the local or state level. Our 8% Problem studies showed that each 8% youth costs the citizens of Orange County an average of $44,000 in custody costs alone. Although incarceration costs are tricky to evaluate because the costs considered will vary and the staffing requirements differ, the $14,000 per case seems like a bargain. The California Youth Authority (state training schools) estimates that it costs $34,000 to house a youth in its institutions annually. We estimate that it costs $41,000 to house a youth in one of our juvenile camps for a year, and at least $54,000 per youth per year in juvenile hall.

Preliminary Experimental Results

Each local ROPP is required to participate in a statewide evaluation by submitting a series of common data elements. Each funded program is also required to have a local program evaluation and to assign eligible cases randomly to experimental and control groups. We have been gathering data on eligible cases assigned to either an experimental or a control group since June 1997. (Appendix F provides a summary of Orange County's research design.)

Some of our funds have been used to develop a research advisory group that enables four of the foremost criminal justice program evaluation experts in the nation to regularly work with us.[6] These researchers also meet periodically with all the county ROPP projects throughout California to provide advice regarding the statewide research effort.

As of June 1999, there were 62 youth assigned to the 8% Early Intervention Program (experimental group) and 57 cases assigned to the control group. Data from the Intake Worksheet and Case Selection Summary used by our officers have been used to evaluate the comparability of these

Table 11.1 The 8% Early Intervention Program: 6- and 12-Month Recidivism Data (All Study Cases)

	6 Months After Program Entry				12 Months After Program Entry			
	Experimental (N = 53)		Control (N = 53)		Experimental (N = 29)		Control (N = 30)	
No. of Subsequent Juvenile Court Petitions Filed	N	% of Total	N	% of Total	N	% of Total	N	% of Total
0	28	53%	24	45%	10	35%	9	30%
1	20	38%	19	36%	13	45%	8	27%
2	5	9%	8	15%	3	10%	6	20%
3 or more	–	–	2	4%	3	10%	7	23%

% of Total With:	Experimental	Control	Experimental	Control
Court Petitions Filed	47%	55%	66%	70%
Warrants Issued	9%	23%	23%	30%[a]
Custody Time (Avg. days in custody)	43% (76)	40% (73)	62% (101)	46% (137)

a. Three (10%) of the control cases tracked for 12 months have outstanding warrants and their whereabouts has been unknown for 3 to 7 months. There are no outstanding warrants on behalf of the experimental cases with 12-month tracking.

Table 11.2 The 8% Early Intervention Program: 6- and 12-Month Recidivism Data (Youth with Juvenile Court Petitions Only)

	6 Months After Program Entry		12 Months After Program Entry	
	Experimental (N = 25)	Control (N =29)	Experimental (N = 19)	Control (N = 21)
Avg. No. of Petitions per Minor	1.2	1.4	1.5	2.0
Avg. No. of New Law Violations per Minor	.6	.6	.7	1.1

two groups. To date, the groups are quite comparable on all the 8% risk factors and other important demographic variables, such as average age, gender and ethnicity.

Fifty-three youth have completed a full 6 months in the 8% Early Intervention Program and 29 program youth have completed 12 months. Likewise, we have been able to follow 53 youth assigned to standard probation services for six months, and 30 control cases for 12 months. Tables 11.1 and 11.2 provide a comparison of recidivism data for the experimental cases at 6 and 12 months with comparable data for the control cases.

There are dramatic differences in the intensity of the services provided the youth in the 8% Early Intervention Program versus the control group. Minors in the demonstration group are all on-site at the YFRC 5 to 6 days per week and receive close supervision and wrap-around services from a multidisciplinary team, whereas the minors in the control group are seen two to four times per month, primarily by the assigned deputy probation officer.

Nonetheless, with the extra attention and monitoring, the 8% program youth have fewer petitions filed for new law violations and, as time goes on, the majority (80%) have had none or one new petition as compared to only 57% for the control cases. This is impressive in that offense data for the control cases is not reported as quickly as that for the 8% program youth and there was a much higher proportion of control youth "in the wind," i.e. with outstanding warrants, for longer periods of time than for the experimental cases.

We are very pleased to see that, with regard to intervening in the progression of 8% problem youth to chronic offender status (i.e. three or more petitions subsequent to court disposition), we appear to be doing substantially better with the experimental group than with the control cases. We are also using the full range of intervention and graduated sanction options.

We are approximately midway in the program evaluation. This study will continue through at least June 2001. These preliminary results, however, are very encouraging. We are seeing program youth attending school, improving social and communication skills, and reducing drug and alcohol use. In addition, parents are participating in the program at a higher level than they were during the field test phase. We also believe that reducing the time lag between the court case disposition and prompt intervention with an array of multidisciplinary services are keys to the positive results we are seeing in program youth.

In the very near future, we will be able to evaluate 6- and 12-month outcome data for the other Repeat Offender Prevention Program counties. While we in Orange County are not declaring "victory" as yet, it is clear that we are on the right track toward an 8% Solution.

Notes

1. Some collaborative partners also have clerical staff located on-site at the YFRC. These clerical staff take turns assisting with receptionist duties.

2. The YFRC was designed to have four classrooms, serving up to 17 students each. Some youth transition to "regular" community schools as part of their program progress or require alternative educational programming, however, such that we may at times only require three classrooms. Having a fourth classroom is recommended because it can be used as a computer lab or to provide additional space for parent education and other group activities during the day.

3. There is also a part-time clinical educator who provides additional health education services for youth and parents.

4. Appendix D provides a written summary of our case selection and other important program procedures. Some of the forms used to gather critical program information can be found on our web site at www.oc.ca.gov/probation.

5. Gendreau, P. (1993, November). The principles of effective intervention with offenders. Paper presented at the International Association of Residential and Community Alternatives, Philadelphia.

6. These research advisory group members include Malcolm Klein, PhD, USC School of Social Science Research Institute; Jim Austin, PhD, formerly director of research for the National Council of Crime and Delinquency and currently a professor at George Washington University; Jill Rosenbaum, criminal justice professor at California State University, Fullerton; and Susan Turner of the RAND Corporation.

12

Overcoming Barriers
8% Lessons Learned

Changing Mind-Sets

One of the greatest barriers to implementing the 8% Early Intervention Program can be the need to change the mind-sets of
those involved. On the program side, everyone involved with the
project, from the field deputies, teachers, counselors, and mentors to the
managers and researchers, must fully understand the unique challenges
posed by this particular group of youthful offenders. Likewise, everyone
involved, including the targeted youth and families, must believe that change
for the better is possible. Being at either end of the spectrum, either overly
optimistic or patently pessimestic, will cause the 8% Early Intervention
Program participants to falter.

Those designing intervention strategies for 8% youth and families and
those implementing programs should acknowledge that what has worked
for them in the past with other youth may not "work" with this group. Staff
will not be asked to jettison their former intervention "tool belts" but will
definitely have to add to them and learn to use them differently.

Most juveniles on probation will eventually comply with court orders
and probation officer directives when faced with the threat of going to juvenile hall or spending their weekends on a work crew. For many 8% minors,
such threats have little or no effect. Most chronic offenders do not fear
juvenile hall and make little or no effort to avoid it. Some actually prefer
the three square meals a day and structured life there compared to the
chaos and poverty at home, the violence on their streets, and having to
watch their backs. This is not to imply that juvenile hall is a pleasant
experience. It is just better than what some of these kids experience day
to day.

What has worked in the past – telling, admonishing, or coaching –
may be initially used by staff. These strategies assume that minors know
how to produce the desired behaviors. Eventually, staff must teach 8%
potential youth and families how to more appropriately respond in given
situations if they want to see behavioral change. We all have learned this
lesson well. A nonprofit agency with expertise working with juvenile of-

fenders learned that using group peer pressure with young, potential 8% youth did not work as well as it did with older, less impulsive teens. These young, multiproblem kids had not developed the social skills or the level of internal control needed to make a positive peer culture work effectively. Kids who have not seen good behavior rewarded appropriately, or bad behavior appropriately punished, make for a poor peer group to evaluate each other's actions.

Limited Resources

In Orange County, as intervention resources became more scarce and violent juvenile crimes increased, we initially felt compelled to pay less attention to minor offenses committed by younger kids and focus more effort on holding older youth, who commit more serious crimes, account-able for their actions. The 8% Problem studies have changed our mind-set. We have seen that this strategy is likely penny-wise and pound-fool-ish.

Now we know which cases to focus on early, regardless of the sever-ity of the crime, and have stopped simply waiting for potential 8% youth to become better criminals by committing additional crimes. Accountability is important, but so are the delinquency indicators that foreshadow a life of more crime. Failing to heed these early warning signs is akin to unplug-ging the "red light" that indicates engine problems in one's car. One can attend to the problem now, or one will likely pay much more dearly later.

If 8% of the juvenile offenders were only responsible for 8% of the repeat crimes, then there would be no need to focus extra attention on them. Because this group is responsible for 55% of repeat offenses, how-ever, it is impossible to ignore them. They fill our juvenile institutions, accounting for the lion's share of our longer term court commitments, and burden the entire juvenile justice system. Worse, they comprise the group that eventually puts more of us in harm's way than any other.

The beauty of the 8% Early Intervention Program is its ability to focus resources on those young people whom the research shows pose the big-gest threat to the safety of our communities. The key is to convince city, county, and state officials that money spent to target these kids and work intensively with their mothers, fathers, and siblings is money well spent.

We have been fortunate in that the people controlling the purse strings locally and in the state legislature believe the 8% Early Intervention Pro-gram is worth pursuing. They have allocated sufficient resources to en-sure that the pilot programs are adequately funded and properly evalu-ated. State welfare reform dollars have been flowing to local probation departments so that we can keep kids and families intact and off of the welfare rolls. Funding for family intervention programming through the expansion of Youth and Family Resource Centers countywide has been a priority for Orange County's share of welfare reform money.

Lessons Learned

The 8% Early Intervention Program is being built on a solid base of research done in Orange County and through linkages with other criminal justice evaluators to help us determine what is more likely to work and what does not work. As with any new venture, however, there are lessons that can be learned only from experience. Every young person in the program, every parent, and every sibling has taught us something. We certainly also benefit from the diverse backgrounds and broad expertise of our program partners.

From Orange County's experience in testing the 8% Early Intervention Program, we have learned the following important lessons:

1. Seek successes early. The most critical phase of the program is the first 30 days, the orientation period. If parents of 8% youth do not see potential benefit to them, they likely will be unwilling to cooperate. The parents should be asked what they believe could assist them and their children to cease committing crimes, and their input needs to be respected. Offers to assist with transportation, child care, or temporary financial aid must be followed through on a timely basis. Unfulfilled promises set up barriers that are difficult to breach. With most 8% families, building a trusting, working relationship will be a slow process. Working together to solve even one problem identified by the minor and family early on can go a long way toward creating a hopeful vision that more successes will follow.

2. Provide close structure and supervision when a youth first enters a program. As each minor demonstrates more internal control, the amount of external control can be reduced. From the outset, rules of behavior need to be clearly defined and appropriately enforced. This will provide an orderly, safe environment for both youth and staff assigned to the program.

3. Accentuate the positive. The flip side to holding youth accountable and delivering consequences is to reward good behavior. Kids must be held accountable, but they respond better to positive reinforcement, particularly over long periods of time. Many of these youth have been hammered with rules and punishment their entire lives, and they have formed a hard shell against what they truly expect to be more of the same. We must search for positives

and reward their achievements, even small ones. It is a success for some youth to simply be ready for school, to get an "A" on a spelling test, or lasting 2 weeks without blurting out an obscenity. Excursions to the beach, to the mountains or fishing trips can be terrific morale boosters. On a daily basis, a reward can be as simple as a break from chores, a soda, or an ice cream cone. One of the most popular rewards for YFRC youth is being the last one picked up in the morning and first one dropped off at home in the afternoon or evening.

4. Create a school environment with clear directions and few distractions. In addition to the consistency of having a van at their front door in the morning, we have a teacher who consistently greets her students with a smile and a handshake each morning before class starts. It is as if to say, "Let's leave our past behind us for now, start this day off on the right foot, and be ready to learn." Consistency does not mean a deadly dull pattern that bores students, however. There must be breaks in the routine for such things as outside presentations, a lively video, a field trip, or an outdoor science experiment. The student who enjoys school will be more eager to return, and perseverance is the key to success. Patience is a requirement for the staff, especially regarding the many 8% youth who are below grade level and struggle with learning disabilities. Any student can be encouraged by finding at least one thing that he or she does well.

5. Stay flexibile. Be creative, and do not be afraid to use individualized approaches. A teacher discovered that merely ignoring a youth's "acting out" worked better than reacting to it in one particular case. When one supervisor says, "This is not math," she recognizes that no formulas exist that work in all cases.

6. Do not make changes in a vacuum. Although experimentation is good, it should not occur in isolation, without the buy-in of the minors, their families, and the collaborative staff. After all, this is a team approach. All oars in the water need to pull in the same direction. One advantage of the weekly staff meetings is to have a feedback loop to determine if changes are working as anticipated. Changes need to have a valid purpose and not be counter to the overall goals of the program or to what the minor or family considers to be important.

7. Communicate. Problems can be dealt with quickly and effectively if the team is aware of what is happening in a family. The entire team, not just a single counselor or probation officer, needs to know. For example, one program youth behaved horribly one morning, got kicked out of the 8% program school for the day, and

refused to participate in a weekend program. We later learned he was suffering emotionally from other problems in his life. He had gotten his girlfriend pregnant and was seeking to get her an abortion. His father, an illegal immigrant with a U.S. prison record, had been deported to Mexico. The young man had just learned that his father was caught trying to return, but instead of being bussed back to the border, was imprisoned as a convicted felon trying to reenter the country. Different staff had known different aspects of the case but had not shared them. As often occurs, the bad behavior was a reflection of internal torment and difficulties at home.

8. Avoid "compassion fatigue." Working with dysfunctional families is mentally, emotionally, and physically draining. Results often fall short of expectations, especially when we try to compare them to our own or "typical" families. We have seen staff become frustrated by setting unrealistic goals for 8% families. Setbacks should not be, but sometimes are, taken personally. Staff members need frequent breaks from these intense involvements to stay healthy. A multidisciplinary team that "backs each other up" in all aspects of service delivery is the best answer to compassion fatigue or staff burn-out.

9. Collaborate, but do not inundate. In one case, a mother complained that she was being asked to schedule meetings with an in-home counselor, a mental health specialist, a drug abuse counselor, and a probation officer and tell them similar information. We quickly rectified that situation, but need to realize that this can happen. Also, at the beginning of the program, parents were asked to sign up to 26 separate release forms. Through collaboration and consolidation, that number was reduced to one.

10. Our efforts are long-term. Expect short-term setbacks. We need to be careful not to give up on 8% youth and families too quickly. We simply cannot effect change without some false starts and slip-ups along the way. These teenagers may very well skip school, run away from home, slip back into drug use, or shoplift during their tenure in the program. We need to learn to celebrate small victories and search for them not just with the teenager on probation but also with his or her brothers, sisters, and parents. Families move forward at their own pace, not necessarily at the pace we would like. We need to develop new mechanisms to track and recognize forward motion.

11. Learn each youth's and family's strengths and build on them. This is a positive and welcomed approach. If a young man struggles in math and science but loves computers, make sure he can learn new computer skills to build on that strength. Perhaps a grand-

mother who lives nearby is a stabilizing influence and hence a strength to the family and can spend more time supervising the children. Search for any "hook" to use to pull a youth or family one step closer to success.

12. Share success: It is contagious. It is easy to find reasons to be discouraged when dealing with these youth and families. Building hope and optimism should be a major program goal for each member of the collaborative team.

13. We will not be successful with everyone. Some may not be ready for serious changes nor want them. The program's agenda and that of a given family may be different, even if they initially buy into the program. Drug and alcohol abuse is an example. Probationers may be willing to hide their drug or alcohol use to the degree they can avoid getting caught but be unwilling to make a total lifestyle change. Even the threat of a probation violation and incarceration may not be enough for some to make needed changes. Often, it takes another compelling reason or catalyst for change, such as mending relations in a family or preparing for school and a career. Some changes may take years to occur. We must not fault ourselves if we provide avenues to get lives on track and individuals choose not to take them.

14. Make community partners. Building good community relations is important and requires ongoing effort. Communities benefit from having truant youngsters off the street and in school and by having those kids who are potentially the greatest threat to community safety under intensive supervision. The "not in my backyard" syndrome, however, remains hard to overcome when searching for a program site. We have had the best success locating sites in areas where we had a broad base of community support beforehand. In these cities, we had made presentations to and sought help from city officials, school districts, youth organizations, local police, and even churches before siting a Youth and Family Resource Center. The local community must also be ready to take these kids back, with summer job possibilities, recreation, or school programs after the intervention programming. We must seek ways to involve the community at every turn.

As we have said, this program and its research is a work in progress. In a few years, we will have learned new lessons, accumulated additional evaluation information, and had more setbacks and successes. This is to be expected when plowing new ground. We learn as much, if not more, than we teach.

13

The Future of the 8% Solution
Building on a Sound Base

We look at a young man such as "Kenny" and feel the same kind of pride that a parent feels when a son or daughter succeeds. In fact, in many ways we served as a surrogate parent for this young man in the year since he joined the 8% Early Intervention Program after his arrest on a graffiti offense.

When he came to us just before his 15th birthday, he was failing his high school classes, smoking marijuana, getting drunk with his buddies, and considered "out of control" at home, where he lived with his mother and stepfather. Since entering the structure of the Youth and Family Resource Center, he is attending school regularly, doing well in academics, and is actually four credits ahead of schedule. He and his family have undergone drug and alcohol abuse counseling with our on-site county health care agency counselor, and he has tested clean of any drug or alcohol use for more than 6 months.

Kenny's parents completed parenting classes conducted in the evenings by our day treatment staff. Life at home, although not perfect, has stabilized. Kenny no longer hangs around the kids with whom he got into trouble, and he got a summer park maintenance job. Most important from a community safety perspective, Kenny has not committed any more criminal offenses to date. In the fall of 1999 he transitioned back to his regular high school. Also, his siblings are on track to finish school and live crime free, which may not have happened had they continued to follow in Kenny's footsteps.

Even with early intervention, there are no guarantees that high-risk youths will remain totally crime free. With these young people, the road to crime-free living is not generally a freeway but more like a winding mountain road with many switchbacks. We have seen program "stars" go through valleys in the rocky road of adolescence as they battle peer pressure and difficulties at home. Some will have to experience out-of-home placement or serve time in custody before achieving a sustained period of law abiding behavior.

The factors contributing to the 8% Problem will not be solved overnight, nor will each factor necessarily resolve at the same time. Years of poor supervision, abuse, bad habits, poverty, family tragedies, and disappointments will rarely be turned around in a few weeks or months, although some positive changes can occur immediately, such as improved school attendance and the resolution of a short-term family crisis. Typically, reducing the risk of reoffending is a building block process in which one success can be followed up by others as new skills and behaviors are learned, practiced, and positively reinforced.

We can provide a wake-up call to a family regarding a son or daughter in distress, help the family prioritize and focus on the most pressing problems, and bring new problem-solving resources to bear. Our involvement in the lives of these high-risk youths and families, however, is at best temporary. The challenge is to empower young people and their parents to develop greater competence and confidence, and we must be willing to begin where they see a need for change. Hope is the essential ingredient for continuing progress on the part of 8% potential youth and parents. We must continually seek to foster it.

There is still much to learn regarding the 8% Solution, and we do not pretend we have all the answers. We are still adding new services, negotiating new contracts with private providers, and revamping old ones. Some services we contracted for in the beginning are now being done "in house" or with new firms. New program sites are being sought countywide. No doubt we will continue to modify the program years into the future as we complete each new research phase. After all, creating cost-effective programs is also a building block process. We are much closer to the 8% Solution than when we first began, however.

This is the direction in which we need to move as juvenile justice agencies. A youngster shoplifting clothes from the mall or spraying graffiti on a neighborhood block wall may simply be committing an isolated act of delinquency. This crime, however, could also be symptomatic of a more extensive set of problems in the young person's life – problems that must be addressed before he or she adopts crime as a pattern in life.

Americans seem to like analogies such as the popular "three strikes and you're out." In the case of serious, repeat crime, it is more like "three strikes and you're in" (prison) for good. The flip side is that for every "third striker" we as a society lock up, another juvenile "first-timer" steps up to the plate for his or her first swing. Is he or she a potential 8% kid who will "strike out"? Maybe yes, maybe no. The good news is we now have a way to determine which kids have that greater potential and we are learning how to help at least some avoid the trip.

Years ago, one of the authors gave a presentation to a group of prosecutors on the 8% Problem research. Also present was an official of the state prison system who, during the question-and-answer period, described the typical state prisoner from his view. He said that the state prisoner is a young man who comes from a disrupted family and is creating a new disrupted family, if he has one. He has a drug or alcohol problem or both and would use them if he could get his hands on them. He is undereducated and underemployed. Look who he is hanging around with – other serious repeat offenders! The prison official said the typical state prisoner is the picture of the 8% kid "grown up." His advice was to either stop the problem in the counties in which they are still a potential 8% Problem or expect to visit them in state prison as "full-blown 8%ers."

We think he is correct. The 8% Solution must be pursued. Allowing these kids to become serious, chronic offenders without trying to stop this pattern is unconscionable both to the families involved and to their victims. Now that we have clearly identified those factors that lead to serious, chronic recidivism with juvenile offenders, we have an obligation to act responsibly before this pattern of criminality becomes set.

We must also face the reality that the juvenile justice system is currently "raising" most of these 8% youth and, unfortunately, "graduating" at least half of them to the adult criminal justice system. If we are even marginally successful in this endeavor, the early intervention program costs will be miniscule compared to the eventual savings in institutional costs and in human pain and suffering. Just think what the possibilities will be for Anita's son and Kenny's grandchildren if they keep their hopes up and persevere.

Appendix A

The "8% Problem": Chronic Juvenile Offender Recidivism

Exploratory Research Findings and Implications for Problem Solutions

Executive Summary

In the 1980s, Orange County, California, experienced a rise in juvenile crime along with a rise in population, increased urbanization, and other changes. Yet the resources available to county and city governments did not keep pace, and sometimes shrank.

As a result, the Orange County Probation Department began focusing its efforts on the most serious offenders, with little left to devote to early intervention. But given limited resources, was this the best approach?

As part of Strategic Planning efforts for the 1990s, the department's management directed its in-house research staff to undertake studies to answer the question, "How well is the Probation Department doing with the youthful offenders of today?" As a by-product of these studies, a group of chronic juvenile re-offenders was identified as the "8% problem."

This report summarizes the significant findings of those exploratory studies, conducted in Orange County between 1987 and 1993.

AUTHOR'S NOTE: This Executive Summary was prepared in March 1994 by Gwen A. Kurz and Louis E. Moore of the Orange County Probation Department to facilitate the distribution of the results of the Probation Department's studies on chronic juvenile offender recidivism to criminal justice professionals and other interested parties. Notations were added by Ms. Kurz in March 1999 to reflect changes resulting from the continuing research effort.

The Probation Department research staff had previously conducted research on risk factors with juvenile offenders and was knowledgeable of other studies in the field. This experience and knowledge provided direction to the formal study effort, which ultimately involved three phases of exploration.

In Study Phase I, two sets of data were examined, each comprising more than 3,000 juvenile offenders who entered Orange County's juvenile justice system for the first time during the first six months of 1985 and 1987, respectively. Each cohort of minors was tracked for three years to determine the overall volume of offenses committed and to examine differences between those minors who commit just one offense versus those who become low rate or chronic re-offenders.

During Study Phase II, a sample of the 1987 study cohort was drawn to further examine the differences between three subgroups:

Non-recidivists: Those minors with one referral to the Probation Department for a criminal offense during the three-year study period.

Low-rate recidivists: Those minors with two or three criminal justice referrals during the three-year study period.

Chronic recidivists: Those minors with four or more referrals during the three-year study period.

For the 1987 study subsamples, researchers gathered additional profile data and extended the tracking period for subsequent offenses to a total of six years.

Study Phase II resulted in a recommended target population for the development and testing of early intervention strategies to reduce chronic juvenile recidivism in Orange County. It also provided data indicative of the costs associated with the "8% problem" group.

In Study Phase III, the specific factors which were found to best predict chronic juvenile offending during Study Phase II were tested with a second, much larger data set. This led to specific recommendations for a pilot intervention project and follow-on study effort.

Overall, these study results are hopeful, concluding that through improved information-sharing and risk assessment techniques, a larger proportion of high-risk minors can be turned around before they become part of the "8% problem." There is also ample evidence that even a small reduction in Orange County's rate of chronic juvenile recidivism can pay major dividends to individual families and the safety of our communities for years to come.

The following provides a summary of the major findings of each study phase and the study conclusions. Also included is a brief description of the "8% problem" solution – the pilot intervention project that is being designed at the Orange County Probation Department.

Study Phase I: "8% Problem" Identification

The tracking of two cohorts of more than 3,000 first-time juvenile offenders revealed that, in the vast majority of cases, the juvenile justice system in Orange County was successful in deterring repeat offenses. Some aspect of each minor's contact with police, probation or the courts apparently had a positive influence on their lives.

On the other end of the spectrum, a small, troublesome group of frequent re-offenders was identified.

More specifically, the study showed that:

1. At least two-thirds of the minors in both studies (71% in the second study) did not have a new probation referral during the initial three-year study period. Referrals to the Probation Department consist of an application for a petition to be filed in Juvenile Court, alleging a criminal offense.

2. Some offenders (21% in the second study) went on to commit one or two additional offenses during the study period.

3. A small percentage of minors (10% in the first study and 8% in the second) committed at least three additional offenses during the study period. These youths accounted for more than half of the repeat offenses committed by each study group.

After the second recidivism analysis was completed on the 1987 cohort, the group of minors with four or more applications for petition during the three-year tracking period began being called the "8% problem" (see Table 1).

Study Phases II and III: "8% Problem" Definition

The next two study phases were aimed at better understanding the characteristics and profile of the "8%" repeat offenders and the costs associated with their handling.

The study effort focused exclusively on the 1987 study group, reexamining the full cohort of 3,164 minors and more in-depth analysis of representative subsamples.

A major conclusion from Study Phase II was that a highly significant proportion of the chronic juvenile offenders in Orange County could be accurately identified and targeted for early intervention at the time of their first-ever system referral. This was done by combining an Age factor (15 or younger at the initial contact) with the presence of a Multi-Problem factor (see Table 2).

Table 1: Orange County Juvenile Justice System
Recidivism Analyses

1985 Cohort Study Results

No. of Referrals per minor during 3-year Tracking Period	No. of Minors In each Category	Percent of Total Minors	No. of Referrals For Each Category	No. of Subsequent Referrals	Percent of Subsequent Referrals
1	2,190	66%	2,190	0	0%
2	541	16%	1,082	541	22%
3	248	8%	744	496	20%
4-14	325	10%	1,771	1,446	58%
Total	**3,304**	**100%**	**5,787**	**2,483**	**100%**

1987 Cohort Study Results

No. of Referrals per minor during 3-year Tracking Period	No. of Minors In each Category	Percent of Total Minors	No. of Referrals For Each Category	No. of Subsequent Referrals	Percent of Subsequent Referrals
1	2,234	71%	2,234	0	0%
2	472	15%	944	472	24%
3	205	6%	615	410	21%
4-14	253	**8%**	1,339	1,086	55%
Total	**3,164**	**100%**	**5,132**	**1,968**	**100%**

Below are the key findings from Study Phases II and III:

1. A majority of the chronic recidivist (8%) group was age 15 or younger at the time of their initial case disposition (57% compared with only 23% and 31% of the non- and low-rate recidivist groups, respectively).

2. Nearly half of the minors who became recidivists were made wards of the Court at their initial system referral versus only 22% of non-recidivists.

3.   The chronic recidivism rate for first-time wards age 15 or less (32%) was four times as great as that of first-time wards age 16 or older (8%). These findings did not vary based on gender, ethnicity, or referral offense.

4.   The chronic recidivist group was found to have significantly more problem areas in their lives, such as drug abuse, dysfunctional families, or failure in school, based on an initial evaluation of six problem variables. These chronic juvenile offenders averaged 3.25 problems each, compared to 1.74 for the low-rate recidivist group and 1.06 for the majority of youths who committed only a single offense. These problem areas were later refined and grouped into the four composite problem factors listed in Table 2.

5. Utilizing the 1987 sub-samples, minors age 15 or less and minors declared wards of the Juvenile Court after their initial offense were also found to have a higher average number of problem factors

(see Table 2) than those who were age 16 or older or whose initial cases were dismissed or handled with informal probation.

6. Based on a six-year follow-up of the1987study sub-samples, chronic juvenile offenders averaged nearly 20 months of incarceration, costing Orange County taxpayers $44,000 apiece in custody costs alone. Because at least 500 new "8% problem" cases are added to Orange County's criminal justice system annually, each new group could potentially cost taxpayers $22 million to incarcerate.

During Study Phases II and III, the researchers also conducted a variety of tests to see how well various factors worked as predictors of youths who would become serious, chronic juvenile offenders.

The previously referenced Multi-Problem profile and Age factors were tested as predictors of chronic recidivism with the study sub-samples from the 1987 cohort. In 70% of the cases, these factors accurately predicted whether a youth would become a chronic juvenile offender. (This test produced 19% false positives and 11% false negatives.) With youths ages 15 and younger, the degree of accuracy rose to 77%, and with older minors it fell to 64%.

In Study Phase III, a similar test was conducted with 905 first-time wards of the court -- the recommended target population and the more serious of the first-time offenders. In 66% of the cases, the recommended factors correctly identified youths as chronic, low rate or non-recidivists. (This test produced 28% false positives and only 6% false negatives.) By correcting problems with variable definitions for the first-time ward data set, the number of false positives can be significantly reduced.

Based on the study results, the authors recommend targeting younger minors with multiple problem profiles as defined in Table 2 for the design of new program strategies aimed at reducing chronic recidivism. Two notes of caution should be considered:

- There is as yet no proof that the recommended strategies (see Study Conclusions) will work better than those currently employed. Therefore, a pilot program is recommended, with a formal program evaluation component.

- The initial target population should consist of young, first-time wards of the Court. The Probation Department already has a mandate to take appropriate action to prevent further criminal activity with this population.

Table 2: Recommended Composite Problem Factors

As defined in the 8% study, the "multi-problem factor" constitutes two or more of the problem factors listed below. For each factor, a "yes" on any one sub-measure constitutes a "problem" in that area. 1999 Note: For the first-time ward population addressed by the 8% Solution, three or more problem factors are required.

   1. School Behavior/Performance Factor

This problem factor consists of three individual measures:

- Attendance Problems (Truancy or a pattern of "skipping" school in certain classes or at certain times of day).
- Behavior Problems (Recent suspensions or expulsion).
- Poor Grades (Failing one or more classes). 1999 Note: Factor now defined as failing two or more classes.

   2. Family Problem Factor

Four individual measures were aggregated to create this factor, each addressing a different dimension.

- Poor Parental Supervision and Control (Parents do not know where the minor goes, what he or she does, or with whom, and have little or no influence in such matters.)
- Significant Family Problems (Illness, substance abuse, recent trauma, major financial problems, marital/family discord or other significant stressors.) 1999 Note: This factor used at Intake only to indicate need for better assessment of family needs or problems subsequent to Intake or court disposition.
- Criminal Family Members Exerting a Negative Influence on the Minor
- Documented Child Abuse or Neglect (Dependent child status or recent petitions filed on the minor's behalf) 1999 Note: This factor now includes family violence.

   3. Substance Abuse Factor

This includes the use of alcohol or drugs by minors in any way but experimentation.

   4. Delinquency Factor

Three measures were included. Each appears associated with a somewhat different criminal pathway, in terms of early onset.

- A Stealing Pattern of Behavior
- A Runaway Pattern of Behavior
- Gang Member or Associate

Study Conclusions

Based on the findings of the entire exploratory research effort, the authors have concluded that:

1. The number of chronic juvenile recidivists in Orange County can be reduced through a coordinated program of aggressive early intervention and treatment of young, high-risk juvenile offenders and their families.

2. A significant proportion of chronic juvenile offenders can be accurately targeted for early intervention the very first time they are referred for juvenile justice system handling. The problems in their lives (from Table 2) are evident before they are influenced by the juvenile justice system or involved in further crimes.

3. Significant risk factors are often overlooked at key points in the processing of youth through Orange County's juvenile justice system due to a lack of critical information. Information-sharing among youth-serving agencies and improved risk assessment techniques hold significant potential for increasing overall system effectiveness.

4. Cooperative, concerted efforts to empower and build the families of high-risk youth can pay major dividends for years to come. More than half of the families of high-risk youth studied for this report had significant problems impeding their ability to provide adequate supervision, structure, or support to their children.

5. Even a modest reduction in recidivism rates for the "8% problem" group identified in this study effort could result in major, long-term savings for Orange County's criminal justice system.

Toward the Development of "8% Problem" Solutions

In the spring of 1993, the Orange County Probation Department was awarded a National Institute of Corrections (NIC) Program Development grant which provides technical assistance from NIC and Temple University staff to design an "8%" intervention program. For the past seven months, a multi-agency group has been meeting to plan the pilot project.

The recommended case identification procedures and assessment tools are currently undergoing field tests. The formal pilot project and research component are expected to be implemented in July 1994.

Key program components will include:

1. Providing adequate levels of supervision, structure, and support to minors and their families throughout the intervention process.

2. Promoting accountability by the minors for their actions and developing increased sensitivity to the impact of their actions on others.

3. Developing strategies that produce educational success, in part by assisting families to ensure that their minors attend school regularly.

4. Promoting pro-social values, behavior and relationships.

5. Developing individualized intervention strategies that are close to home and have strong follow-up beyond the "crisis" stage.

6. Strongly promoting teamwork among the family, professional staff, and community volunteers.

1999 Note: Due to Orange County's declaration of bankruptcy in December 1994, the field tests were continued into 1996. Based on the field test results, the validity of the theoretical model was confirmed. However, a number of process issues and critical program resources were identified as important for sustaining short-term positive program outcomes, i.e., for the first 6-12 months of wardship, in the longer term, e.g. to curtail serious, chronic juvenile offending and prevent the development of adult criminal careers.

Through a combination of local, state and federal funds, the proposed 8% Problem Solution was implemented with the desired formal experimental research component in June 1997. This demonstration program/research project will continue through June 2001.

Appendix B

8% Problem Study Methodology

Background

Over the decade of the 1980s, the County of Orange became increasingly urban and more ethnically and culturally diverse. Statistics published by the County Administrative Office indicate that from 1980 to 1990:

- The total population of Orange County increased by 26%.

- The number of cities in Orange County grew to 31, with 10 over 100,000 population and five new since 1988.

- The Hispanic population of Orange County doubled while its Asian population tripled. By 1990, one in four Orange County residents was Hispanic, while one in 10 was Asian.

- 7,400 undocumented aliens were added each year for a total of 166,000 by 1990.

Over the same time period, there was dramatic growth in the number of criminally active gangs, violent crimes, and crimes involving the use of weapons. Many of these serious crimes have involved juvenile offenders. Information provided by the California Center for Law Enforcement Assistance indicated that, from 1980 to 1990, juvenile arrests for violent crimes increased by 45% – murder +130%, forcible rape +70%, and robbery +65% – while juvenile felony arrests involving the use of weapons increased by 48%.

The resources available to county and city governments to deal with the problems and challenges of increased urbanization could not keep pace. The trend was, therefore, to focus a greater proportion of available

AUTHOR'S NOTE: This is a composite of the background section and original appendix from *The "8% Problem": Chronic Juvenile Offender Recidivism* (Kurz and Moore, 1994) which describes the research methodology used to examine juvenile offender recidivism in Orange County.

resources on the most difficult urban problems. Within the juvenile justice system of Orange County, as the number of referrals for serious crimes increased, the demand for programs and services that ensure a higher level of community protection also increased. According to the records of the Orange County Probation Department, from 1980 to 1990 Juvenile Court dispositions involving custody increased by 43%, commitments to local institutions were up 40%, and commitments to the California Youth Authority rose by 169%.

These higher control dispositional options are very costly. In 1990, local commitments in Orange County averaged 74 days and cost approximately $5,500 each, whereas commitments to the California Youth Authority averaged just over two years and cost about $55,000 per commitment. If a minor receives multiple commitments at any level, the custody costs alone become staggering![1]

Noting these disturbing trends, between 1985 and 1987 the Orange County Probation Department implemented a model for the management of probation resources recommended by the National Institute of Corrections (NIC). This model is predicated on the use of valid procedures for assessing the relative degree of risk various groups of minors present for committing multiple offenses. Therefore, as part of model implementation, the department developed and validated a Juvenile Offender Risk Assessment instrument, with technical assistance from the federal Office of Juvenile Justice and Delinquency Prevention and NIC staff.

Developed for use with a probation field supervision population, the instrument was initially constructed utilizing those factors that juvenile field supervision officers felt best predicted subsequent offense behavior. Data was collected on both new and active cases to test the proposed Initial Assessment and Reassessment instruments. This sample of over 500 cases was followed for a six-month period and any subsequent petition filings recorded. These included both alleged technical and new law violations.

Based on these data analyses, the Orange County classification instruments were fine-tuned to achieve maximum discrimination[2] based on the dependent variables, i.e., the number of new law and technical violations over an initial six-month tracking period. The following factor sets were found to differentiate High-, Medium-, and Low-Risk juvenile probationers in Orange County, in order of their relative contribution to a higher risk of reoffending.

PRIOR OFFENSE HISTORY: Multiple measures, ranging from prior arrests up to and including prior incarceration or out-of-home placement. (The more "priors," the higher the risk score.)

MULTIPLE PROBLEMS: Includes lack of parental supervision and control; school attendance, behavior, and/or performance problems; substance abuse; chronic runaway behavior; and gang affiliations. (The more problems, the higher the Risk score.)

AGE AT INITIAL ASSESSMENT (15 or younger vs. 16 and older): This factor proved to be important in relation to the other two factor sets, particularly, the problem variables referenced above. (Younger minors with multiple problems had significantly higher recidivism rates than their older counterparts in both the Medium- and High-Risk groups.)

When these Juvenile Offender Risk Assessment instruments were formally adopted by the Probation Department and placed into departmentwide use, a Management Information System component was also established to record the profile of each minor at the Initial and most recent (or, Final) Assessment and document all technical and new law violations occurring during each minor's period of supervision. Thus, the capability was created to monitor and test the validity of these classification instruments, both over time and for longer periods of offense tracking than those utilized in the original validation effort.

8% Problem Identification

In late 1988, a department-wide strategic planning effort was launched aimed at preparing for the anticipated changes and challenges in Orange County during the decade of the 1990s. Among the first questions raised by the participating managers were:

- How are "we" – the Orange County Probation Department – doing with the youthful offenders of today?

- Does the historical effectiveness information provide any clues as to how the department needs to change its service delivery systems to be more effective with the youthful offender populations of the next decade?

A significant amount of information was available on the outcomes achieved by individual program components administered by the department, such as the County's Juvenile Diversion program, probation field supervision and institutional treatment programs. However, there was very little information available by which to gauge the effectiveness of the department's overall juvenile operation or the relative costs of serving minors who re-offend with different frequencies.

In this latter regard, one data set offered some promise -- the Juvenile Court and Probation Statistical System (JCPSS) maintained by the California Bureau of Criminal Statistics (BCS). While containing a somewhat limited set of information,[3] the Orange County data were both complete and known to be of consistently high quality, thanks to the efforts of both

BCS and departmental clerical staff over the years of the JCPSS' existence.

In 1989 and again in 1990, two recidivism analyses were completed with assistance from the California Bureau of Criminal Statistics. Both involved the identification of an entire cohort of minors with their "first ever" application for petition during the first six months of either 1985 or 1987. In both study efforts, the number of minors identified equated to more than 3,000 individuals.

The 1985 cohort was tracked through the end of 1987 (and the 1987 cohort was tracked through the end of 1989) to identify:

1. Any minors having subsequent applications for petition within each three-year study period; and

2. The number and proportion of minors with 1, 2, 3 etc. subsequent applications for petition within each three-year tracking period.

The cohort was divided into three study groups stratified according to the total number of times minors were referred to the Probation Department during the tracking period.

The first study group included those minors who had only one application for petition during the entire tracking period. This group accounted for 71% of the cohort (2,234 of 3,164) and is referred to as the Non-recidivist study group.

The second study group (677 of 3,164) consisted of minors who had a total of two or three applications for petition during the follow-up period. This group comprised 21% of the study cohort and accounted for 45% of all re-referrals during the follow-up period. This group of minors is referred to as the Low-Rate recidivist group.

The third and final group included minors with a total of four or more applications for petition during the tracking period and is referred to as the Chronic recidivist (or "8% problem") group. These minors comprised only 8% of the study cohort, but accounted for 55% of all re-referrals during the tracking period.

Problem Definition
(Relationship to Juvenile Risk Factors)

Having identified this "8% problem" group, the next phase of data exploration was aimed at broader definition of the problem, using the authors' knowledge of juvenile offender risk prediction factors to guide the analysis plan.

Noting that the department does not appear to be doing well with its "8%-ers" now, the specific study questions were:

1. Are the "8%" minors different from the other two groups of non- and low-rate juvenile recidivists in ways that can be accurately and consistently identified <u>early</u> in their careers (at the first or second system referral)?

2. Is there anything in the data regarding the profile or current handling of these "8%" minors that would provide us with clues as to problem solutions (i.e., more cost-effective intervention strategies and/or ways of allocating limited juvenile justice system resources)?

There were five steps involved in acquiring the study sample used for this analysis phase, once the 1987 study cohort had been partitioned into the three study groups described in Section II.

Step 1 required reducing the original 1987 cohort by 49 cases, to exclude those cases that were missing any of the original JCPSS data elements. (In this process, the proportional relationships between the original study groups were maintained.)

In Step 2, a sample of 220 minors was initially selected, using age distributions as the criteria to determine the appropriate sample size for each of the three study groups. Three subsamples were selected, one from each of the total cohort study groups, including 78 Non-recidivists, 70 Low-Rate Recidivists, and 72 Chronic Recidivists.

Steps 3 and 4 of the sample development process required a thorough review of the juvenile case files for each of the cases selected in Step 2. Step 3 confirmed that only minors with initial referrals during the first six months of 1987 were assigned to the study sample. Step 4 verified the number of system contacts during the initial tracking period. (This step included tracking minors into the adult system if they turned 18 during the 36-month follow-up period.) As a result of these two sample development steps, 13 cases were deleted from the study sample and 42 cases were reassigned to a different study group, as follows.

*   22% of the non-recidivist cases were found to be Low-Rate recidivists and 5% were found to be Chronic recidivists. (73% remained in the Non-recidivist subgroup.)

*   4% of the original Low-Rate recidivists became Non-recidivists while 22% were found to be Chronic recidivists. (74% remained in the Low-Rate recidivist group.)

*   None of the Chronic recidivists were moved to the Non-recidivist group while 6% were found to be Low-Rate recidivists. (94% remained in the Chronic recidivist group.)

Without this case review process, the size of the Non-recidivist group would have been overstated while the size of the Low-Rate and Chronic recidivist groups would have been understated.

During Step 5, the residence status of each minor was verified. As a result, a total of 36 cases were removed from the study sample due to being out-of-county residents.

Thirty-six percent of the Non-recidivist cases were out-of-county residents vs. 16% of the Low-Rate recidivists and a mere 6% of the Chronic recidivist subgroups.

The following chart provides a comparison of the original study sample with the one ultimately used for the follow-up study analyses:

Table 1: 8% Study Sample Development

	Step 2: Original Sample (N = 220)	Step 3: Removal of Cases Not in Study Time Frame (N = 207)	Step 4: Adjusted Group (N = 207)	Step 5: Removal of Out Of County Cases (N = 171)
Non-Recidivist Subsample	78 (35%)	73 (35%)	56 (27%)	36 (21%)
Low-Rate Recidivist Subsample	70 (32%)	67 (32%)	69 (33%)	58 (34%)
Chronic Recidivist Subsample	72 (33%)	67 (33%)	82 (40%)	77 (45%)

From this sample selection process involving detailed case reviews, the authors concluded that the original "8% problem" designation might understate the chronic recidivism rate for juveniles initially referred to the juvenile justice system in Orange County. The actual rate may be somewhat higher, but would not be expected to exceed 15%.

First-time Ward Data Set (N = 905)

The 1987 Referral Cohort Study subsample analyses provided valuable information regarding the relationship between the identified problem factors, the minor's age and subsequent wardship status, and chronic juvenile offender recidivism rates. One limitation, particularly as related to the "multiproblem" factor testing, was the size of the study subsamples. Therefore, before moving ahead to develop intervention strategies for first-time wards with the identified high-risk profiles, the authors felt the need to "test" the predictive accuracy of the recommended target population "eligibility criteria" with a larger sample of first-time wards.

The Orange County Probation Department maintains a Management Information System component called the Juvenile Profile/Outcome System, which consists of the profile of each minor placed under field supervision at the time of his or her initial and most recent (or final) assessment for case classification purposes. This database was used to identify a one-year cohort of "first-time" juvenile wards, i.e., those with no prior arrests or referrals to the Probation Department in Orange County during CY-1987. A total of 1,039 cases were initially identified who met these selection criteria.

Cases from this group of first-time wards were then matched to their corresponding records in the JCPSS data file. 905 of the 1,039 first-time wards selected from the Juvenile Profile/Outcome system were found to also have complete records in the 1987 JCPSS data file. This cohort of 905 minors (referred to as the First-time Ward data set) was further partitioned into three subsamples, based on the total number of times the minor was referred on an application for petition during the three-year follow-up period.

Within the First-time Ward data set, 50% of the cases (450/905) were found to be Non-recidivists, 35% (315/905) were found to be Low-Rate recidivists (having one or two subsequent petitions during the three-year follow-up period) and 15% (140/905) were identified as Chronic recidivists with a total of four or more petitions during the three-year follow-up period.

In order to investigate the relationship between the previously identified problem factors and chronic juvenile offender recidivism rates, variables from the Orange County Juvenile Offender Risk and Needs Assessment scales were selected which most closely approximated the 8% risk factor definitions. These data were then subjected to the statistical analyses described in the text of this report.

Study Limitations/8% Exploratory Areas
for Additional Study

As with any study dealing with risk prediction, the extent to which the 8% Problem study findings and conclusions may be generalized to other jurisdictions of comparable size and demographic make-up (much less those which are noncomparable) is an issue that should be approached with caution.

A number of other jurisdictions in California have used the Orange County Probation Department's recidivism analysis methodology to see what they come up with in terms of non-, low-rate, and chronic recidivist groups. This was, in fact, part of the technical assistance grant jointly awarded by the National Institute of Corrections to the Orange and Los Angeles County Probation Departments to assist in the design of potential "8% problem" solution(s) in these two counties.

The specific risk factors that were used in the development of the Orange County pilot intervention project, i.e. field test, and case identification procedures are comparable to those which other researchers have found to be significantly correlated with a higher risk of reoffending. They have nonetheless been specifically developed to accurately identify the youth in Orange County's juvenile justice system referral and/or ward population that are in need of a high level of resource coordination and focus.

Additionally, most of the proposed risk assessment variables have been validated and revalidated with various juvenile offender populations in Orange County over the past 10 years. Thus, the goal of the 1987 Initial Referral sample data analyses was not to create a new risk scale, but to confirm that the study subsamples conformed to the anticipated variable distribution patterns and to determine which factors best predict chronic juvenile offending.

The focus of the initial pilot project (or "field test") aimed at improving Orange County's "system batting average" with chronic juvenile recidivists was, as previously stated, younger, first-time wards in Orange County who present a multiproblem profile at the time of their first (or second) system referral. This is primarily because, based on the Orange County data analyses, this group had the highest rate of chronic recidivism. However, the authors wish to emphasize that we do not advocate, nor do any of our study findings support, any type of punitive action or the exercise of a higher level of control over the minor's actions based on the recommended target population criteria, than those already mandated or authorized by the Court in each individual case.

Further testing of the recommended "8%" case identification procedures has occurred and is still occurring to refine the estimates of the number of new "8%" minors that the system can be expected to receive in coming years. Major improvements have also been made in assessing the risk and needs associated with all first-time wards on a more timely and accurate basis and expediting the initiation of appropriate intervention programming.

System cost estimates need to be refined, using measures other than custody time savings. In the current experimental program evaluation, consultation with the County Executive Office and other juvenile justice system professionals is taking place to more fully address this important measure of project impact.

Under a separate state grant, the authors are also testing an early intervention program for older, first-time wards who become chronic recidivists. The analyses conducted to date indicate that substance abuse may be the most significant factor in the "late" onset of a chronic pattern of re-offending for this 8% problem group.

From the case study portion of this study effort, the authors were impressed with what appears to be a link between younger minors whose profile at initial referral includes a pattern of runaway behavior and child abuse/neglect. Unfortunately, this latter issue is often not recognized (nor does it come to the system's attention) until years after the initial system referral; however, minors subsequently report it as a long-standing issue, related to their earlier runaway episodes. This area is receiving closer attention in the pilot project case assessment, service delivery, and follow-on study plans.

Notes

1.   Local custody cost data provided by the Orange County Probation Department. State custody cost data provided by the California Youth Authority.

2.   Baird, C. (1984, March) Review of Orange County Juvenile Probation Classification System. Isthmus Associates. Madison, Wisconsin.

3.   The Juvenile Court and Probation Statistical System (JCPSS) database consisted of all minors referred for alleged criminal code violations for which the disposition of that offense occurred within a given calendar year. The database includes the minor's name, date of birth, gender, ethnicity, the highest referral charge – both the level (felony vs. misdemeanor) and type (criminal code section) – and all system disposition data and dates, e.g., Probation, District Attorney and Court, related to each discrete referral. The statewide system was terminated in October 1990, due to budget cutbacks at the state level. Efforts to bring this system back on line are currently under way. Orange County has maintained this database locally to the present time.

Appendix C

California Repeat Offender Prevention Project
Common Program Components

1. Common Target Population Definition

- First-time wards of the Juvenile Court for criminal charges, living at home and under probation supervision, less than age 15.5 at time of wardship and presenting at least three 8% risk factors. (Before July 1999, Los Angeles County Probation was testing this early intervention approach with youth who had not as yet come in contact with the juvenile justice system for criminal offenses. However, all seven counties now use the same target population definition.)

2. Common Program Elements

- Multi-disciplinary assessment and service delivery approach aimed at empowering potential 8% youth and families to solve problems in identified 8% risk factor areas through intensive intervention (competency building) efforts.

- The use of a broader range of graduated sanctions, encouraging 8% youth to accept responsibility for their criminal actions.

3. Common Program Goals

- To reduce the number of high-risk youth who become serious, chronic juvenile and adult offenders.

- To reduce the demand for long-term custody commitments on behalf of the target population.

AUTHOR'S NOTE: This summary of program components was extracted from materials prepared by the California Board of Corrections for the participating counties in the California Repeat Offender Prevention Project. The program components were derived from the enabling legislation. The applicable sections of the state's Welfare and Institutions Code are also included.

4. Common Program Evaluation Framework

- Data collection and analysis involving an experimental research design and employing random assignment of youth and families meeting the program selection criteria to an experimental program or control group. (The expectation is that the services provided to the experimental program group will be substantially different, such as of greater intensity and duration, than those provided to the control group.)

Pilot counties were encouraged to develop a program implementation strategy that best meets the needs of their respective target populations to access and benefit from model program services. Those strategies must take into account necessary differences in juvenile justice system policies, procedures and resources.

Repeat Offender Prevention Project

State of California
Welfare & Institutions Code

ARTICLE 18.5
REPEAT OFFENDER PREVENTION PROJECT
(Added by Stats 1994 ch 730 §1, eff. 111195)
(See other Article 18.5 above.)

§743. Repeat Offender Prevention Project.
Contingent upon the appropriation of funds therefor, there is hereby established a three-year pilot project which shall be known as the "Repeat Offender Prevention Project." This project shall operate in the Counties of Fresno, Humboldt, Los Angeles, Orange, San Diego, San Mateo, and Solano, and the City and County of San Francisco, unless the board of supervisors of one or more of these counties adopts a resolution to the effect it will not participate in the project, each of which shall either design, establish, implement, and evaluate a model program to meet the needs of a juvenile offender population identified as having the potential to become repeat serious offenders utilizing the findings of exploratory studies conducted in Orange County between 1989 and 1993 by the research staff of the Orange County Probation Department and which identified certain minors who were designated as the "8 percent" population. The main goal of this Program is to develop and implement a cost-effective multi-agency, multidisciplinary program which targets youth displaying behavior that may lead to delinquency and recidivism. *(Added by Stats 1994 ch 730 §1; amended by Stats 1996 ch 1049 §1; Stats 1998 ch 327 §1, eff. 1/1/99.)*

§744. Administration; application for funding.
(a) The Repeat Offender Prevention Project shall be administered by the Board of Corrections and each program shall be under the onsite administration of the chief probation officer in the county selected for participation in the project or under a consortium of chief probation officers representing each participating county.

(b) Pursuant to this article, a chief probation officer or the regional consortium, with the approval of the appropriate board or boards of supervisors, may apply to the Board of Corrections for funding to implement a program meeting the criteria specified in subdivision (b) of Section 745. The goal of each program shall be to develop and demonstrate intervention strategies which will end each participating minor's escalating pattern of criminal and antisocial behavior, a pattern that leads to chronic delinquency and, potentially, to adult criminal careers. These strategies shall be provided within the parameters of community protection and offender accountability. Application for program funding shall be made in accordance with written guidelines established by the Board of Corrections in consultation with chief probation officers throughout the state. *(Added by Stats 1994 ch 730 §1; amended by Stats 1998 ch 32 7§2, eff. 1/1/99.)*

§745. Program participation guidelines.
The Board of Corrections shall establish goals and deadlines against which the success or failure of the program demonstration projects may be measured. The board shall also develop selection criteria and funding schedules for participating counties which shall take into consideration, but not be limited to, all of the following:
(1) Size of the eligible target population as defined in Section 746.
(2) Demonstrated ability to administer the program.
(3) Identification of service delivery area.
(4) Demonstrated ability to provide or develop the key intervention strategies described in Section 748 to the eligible target population and their families.
(5) A formal research component utilizing an experimental research design and random assignment to the program. *(Added by Stats 1994 ch 730 §1; amended by Stats 1996 ch 1049 §2; Stats 1998 ch 327 §3. eff. 1/1/99.)*

§746. Qualifications for participating minors.
A minor shall be selected for participation in a program established pursuant to this article based upon the following factors:
(a) The minor is 15½ years of age or younger, has been declared a ward of the juvenile court for the first time and is to be supervised by a probation department selected for participation in this project.
(b) The minor has been evaluated and found to have at, least three of the following factors, that place the minor at a significantly greater risk of becoming a chronic juvenile or adult offender:
(1) School behavior and performance problems. This shall include at least one of the following: attendance problems; school suspension or expulsion; or failure in two or more academic classes during the previous six months or comparable academic period.
(2) Family problems. These shall include at least one of the following: poor parental supervision or control; documented circumstances of domestic violence; child abuse or neglect; or family members who have engaged in criminal activities.
(3) Substance abuse. This shall include any regular use of alcohol or drugs by the minor, other than experimentation.
(4) High-risk predelinquent behavior. This shall include at least one of the following: a pattern of stealing, chronic running away from home; or gang membership or association.
(5) The minor matches the at-risk profile for becoming a chronic and repeat juvenile offender according to the criteria developed by the Multi-Agency At-Risk Youth Committee (MAARYC). *(Added by Stats 1994 ch 730§1; amended by Stats 1996 ch 1049 §3; Stats 1998 ch 327 §4, eff. 1/1/99.)*

§747. Minimum standards and commitment.
The Board of Corrections shall adopt written minimum standards for project implementation, operation, and evaluation which shall include a written commitment by a county or region to the following objectives:
(a) Teamwork on the part of all treatment and intervention agents involved in the project including the family, the professionals, and any community volunteers.
(b) Empowerment of the family to recognize and, ultimately, to solve the problems related to their

minor's delinquent behavior and their involvement as an integral part of the treatment team and process.

(c) Creation of a multiagency, multidisciplinary, and culturally competent team so that the program can effectively draw on the professional knowledge, skill, and experience of many treatment disciplines in areas including, but not limited to, the following: education; job preparation and search; job skills and vocational training; life skills; psychological counseling; mental health services; drug and alcohol treatment; health care; parenting skills; community service opportunities; building self-esteem and self-confidence; mentoring programs; restitution programs; gang intervention; crime prevention; recreational, social, and cultural activities; and transportation and child care as needed. *(Added by Stats 1994 ch 730 §l; amended by Stats 1996 ch 1049 §4; Stats 1998 ch 32 7 §5, eff 1/1/99.)*

§748. Intervention strategies.

Each county or region shall, in implementing their respective programs, provide the following key intervention strategies to ensure the following:

(a) Adequate levels of supervision, structure, and support to minors and their families both during and after the intervention and treatment process, in order to accomplish the following:

(1) Ensure protection of the community, the minor, and his or her family.

(2) Facilitate the development of new patterns of thinking and behavior.

(3) Eliminate any obvious stumbling blocks to the family's progress.

(4) Facilitate the development of enhanced parenting skills and parent-child relationships.

(b) Accountability on the part of the minor for his or her actions and assistance to the minor in developing a greater awareness and sensitivity to the impact of his or her actions on both people and situations.

(c) Assistance to families in their efforts to ensure that minors arc attending school regularly.

(d) Assistance to the minor in developing strategies for attaining and reinforcing educational success.

(e) Promotion and development of positive social values, behavior, and relationships by providing opportunities for the minor to directly help people; to improve his or her community; to participate in positive leisure-time activities specially chosen to match his or her individual interests, skills, and abilities; and to have greater access and exposure to positive adult and juvenile role models.

(f) Promotion of partnerships between public and private agencies to develop individualized intervention strategies which shall include, but not be limited to, the following:

(1) Delivery of services in close proximity to the minor's or the minor's family's home.

(2) Community case advocates to assist in building bridges of trust, communication, and understanding between the minor, the family, and all treatment and intervention agents.

(g) Provision of a continuum of care with strong followup services that continue to be available to the minor and family as long as needed, not just on a crisis basis. *(Added by Stats 1994 ch 730 §1; amended by Stats 1996 ch 1049 §5; Stats 1998 ch 327 §6, eff. 1/1/99.)*

§749. Program progress reports.

(a) The Board of Corrections shall be responsible for monitoring demonstration project and expansion program implementations in accordance with an annual program plan submitted by the participating counties or regions. Written progress and evaluation reports shall be required of all participating counties pursuant to a schedule and guidelines developed by the Board of Corrections.

(b) The success of each funded demonstration project shall be determined, at a minimum, by comparing a control group, consisting of juvenile offenders who were not selected for participation in the project, to an experimental group, consisting of juvenile offenders who have participated in the project. Juveniles in each group shall be evaluated at 6-, 12-, 18-, and 24-month intervals, according to the following criteria:

(1) The number of subsequent petitions to declare the minor a ward of the juvenile court, pursuant to Section 602, and the subject matter and disposition of each of those petitions.

(2) The number of days served in any local or state correctional facilities.

(3) The number of days of school attendance during the current or most recent semester.

(4) The minor's grade point average for the most recently completed school semester.

(c) The Board of Corrections, based on reports provided pursuant to subdivision (a), shall report upon request to the Legislature on the effectiveness of these programs in achieving the demonstration project and program goals described in this article.

(d) The Board of Corrections shall determine county or regional eligibility for funding and, from money appropriated therefor, the board shall allocate and award funds to those counties or regions applying and eligible therefor and selected for project participation.

(c) The Repeat Offender Prevention Project shall be implemented within six months of the appropriation of funds therefor and shall terminate at the end of three years from that appropriation.

(f) Five percent of the funds allocated each fiscal year for the Repeat Offender Prevention Project shall be set aside for the administrative expenses of the Board of Corrections. *(Added by Stats 1994 ch 730 §1; amended by Stats 1998 ch 327 §7, eff. 1/1/99.)*

Appendix D

Case Selection and
Program Process Summary
8% Early Intervention Program

Juvenile Probation Intake

Minors may be referred to the Probation Department for Intake as either Noncustody or Custody cases. Noncustody cases remain in the community during the processing of their offense behavior, while custody cases are lodged in Juvenile Hall. In either situation, the case may receive a full intake or be sent directly to the District Attorney for filing without benefit of an intake. The following briefly describes the handling of each type of case:

Cases receiving full intakes: Minors who receive full intakes will be interviewed by an Intake officer and will have the opportunity to provide a statement concerning the circumstances of the offense as well as information about themselves including social history, school performance, substance use, etc. The parents will also be interviewed. Following completion of the interview, the Intake officer will complete an Intake Assessment Worksheet which summarizes the case and identifies potential problems in four key areas associated with chronic delinquency (i.e., family issues, school issues, substance abuse, and delinquency

---

AUTHOR'S NOTE: This is an Orange County Probation Department internal document prepared by research and program staff. It was designed to document the case selection process and other key program processes for the purpose of staff training and for program replication in other county regions.

factors). If the Intake officer identifies two or more problems, then the case is flagged as a "potential 8% case." (Risk Verification Criteria and Guidelines are used by Intake, Investigation and Case Screening personnel to assess the 8% Risk Factors).

<u>Cases with no intakes:</u> If the minor and his/her parents fail to appear for their scheduled appointments for interviews, the case will automatically be referred to the District Attorney for filing and no Intake Assessment will be completed. The Application for Petition is the only source of information regarding the case.

<u>653 WIC cases sent directly to the DA without intake:</u> Welfare and Institutions Code section 653 requires that minors who commit offenses defined under this code section are sent directly to the District Attorney for filing without benefit of a Probation Intake. In these cases, involving more serious crimes, no Intake Assessment Worksheet will be completed. There will also be no interview with the minor nor his/her parents or guardians. The Application for Petition is the only source of information regarding the case.

Juvenile Investigation

If ordered by the Court, the Juvenile Investigation function will complete a report which will include a summary of the offense, the minor's offense history, a social history if the minor's parents or guardians are available for interview, a victim statement if appropriate, a statement from the minor, and a recommendation regarding disposition of the case. Court reports are not ordered for every case.

Aftercourt

The juvenile case file is forwarded to the Aftercourt function following Court disposition and declaration of wardship. The Aftercourt function is responsible for routing the case file to the appropriate area office following completion of the case file setup process. The Aftercourt clerk will screen each of the cases coming through the function and will flag those cases meeting the following criteria and forward them to the 8% Early Intervention Project Supervisor at the Youth and Family Resource Center in Anaheim:

- The minor is a newly declared ward
- The minor was 15 and 6 months or younger on the date of wardship declaration
- The minor lives in the cities of Anaheim, Buena Park, or Fullerton

Case Screening

The Supervisor of the 8% Early Intervention Program or designee is responsible for screening each of the flagged cases to determine their eligibility for the program. The screening will involve a review of the documents that are available in the case file. The documents may include the:

- Intake Assessment Worksheet
- Application for Petition
- Dispositional Report, if one was completed
- Court Order, including the terms and conditions of probation
- The Police report

If there is no Dispositional Report in the file, the screener (a probation officer) will call the Juvenile Investigation Unit to determine if one was completed and, if so, have a copy of the report faxed to the Youth and Family Resource Center to expedite the screening process.

In addition, the screener will contact the Social Services Agency to obtain information regarding the family's history of contacts with the agency including incidence of 300 WIC (dependency) petitions, child abuse reports (CAR), or other contacts. The information is generally available immediately through a computerized records system and will be faxed to the screener.

The screener may obtain other information including school records and social history information through contacts with the family members.

The case screener will complete a Case Selection Summary packet that identifies characteristics that are associated with a pattern of chronic recidivism.

In order to be eligible for the program, the minor must meet the following criteria:

1. The minor has been declared a ward of the Juvenile Court as a result of a first or second filed petition to the Probation Department.

2. The minor is 15.5 years of age or younger at the point of declaration of wardship.

3. The minor resides in the target area (i.e., the cities of Anaheim, Buena Park or Fullerton).

4. The minor has three or more of the problems identified through Case Selection Summary that suggest that he or she may be at risk for chronic recidivism:

   • Poor school behavior or performance (may include truancy suspensions or expulsions, and/or failing grades)
   • Chronic family problems (predominantly identified by a lack of adequate parental supervision, structure, and support for pro-social activities)
   • Drug or alcohol use (any pattern of use, regardless of amount)
   • Pre-delinquent factors (includes a pattern of running away from home, a history of stealing, and/or identification with gang members or association with criminally involved peers)

5. The minor is a legal resident of the State of California.

If the minor is found to meet these criteria, the case will be referred to the Research staff for a case assignment determination. This will be accomplished via telephone or direct contact with the Research staff. The case file will remain with the screener until a determination is made.

Minors who do not meet the eligibility criteria will be forwarded to a regular juvenile field supervision unit.

The case screening process will be completed within 3 working days of the receipt of the case by the case screener.

Case Assignment

Eligible cases will be randomly assigned to either the 8% Repeat Offender Prevention Project (experimental) or regular juvenile field supervision (control) by the Research staff. The 8% Repeat Offender Prevention Program (ROPP) SPO will forward all case screening forms to the Research staff.

ROPP cases: If the minor is assigned to the 8% ROPP, the Unit Supervisor will assign the case to one of 4 DPOs.

Control cases: If the minor is assigned to the control group, the case file will be forwarded to the North County Field Services Office for assignment by the regular field supervision Unit SPO.

The case screener will forward each case with a packet of forms that are to be completed by the assigned DPO. These forms include

• A school release form
• A Family Assessment form

Case Assessment

The case assessment for both experimental and control cases will involve the completion of the following:

• Initial Risk/Needs Assessment
• Initial Family Assessment
• Case Plan

The assessment process is to be completed within 45 days of the assignment of the case. In order to gather necessary information to complete the assessment and develop a case plan, the assigned DPO will review all of the available records, complete one or more interviews with the minor and his/her family, and visit the minor's home. The forms that will be used for the assessment of the minor and family in the experimental and control groups are identical. The case planning forms and process differ, however.

Control group: Following assessment of the minor's risk and needs factors, the DPO will complete the objective-based case plan section of the Initial Risk/Needs Assessment packet. This will include identification of specific case objectives and an action plan to achieve those objectives. The case plan will be reviewed by the Supervising Probation Officer and issues of concern will be staffed with the DPO.

Experimental group (8% Early Intervention Program): During the 45-day assessment period the assigned DPO will have frequent contact with the minor and the family at the Youth and Family Resource Center as well as at their home. Treatment team members will also be involved in contacts with the family to develop a thorough assessment of the minor and family's needs. During this period, complete school records will be obtained on the minor and any available diagnostic information will be requested.

A meeting will be scheduled for the minor and family and the treatment team at approximately the 45-day point to develop a mutually agreeable case plan. Two weeks prior to this meeting, the treatment team will meet to discuss the problems that the minor and parents shared and the issues the team members observed and will begin to develop some preliminary ideas about how to address the needs of the minor and family. The case planning meeting will be a shared discussion of these issues with the family so that a consensus can be achieved regarding the case plan. The following individuals may be involved in the development of the case plan, though in the interest of not overwhelming the minor and parents, not all may be present for the case-planning meeting:

• Minor
• Parents
• 8% Deputy Probation Officer (DPO)
• 8% Supervising Probation Officer (SPO)
• Deputy Probation Counselor(s)
• Department of Education staff
• Intensive in-home services
• Mental Health staff
• Social Services staff
• Drug/alcohol abuse services staff
• Health care staff

• Community resource collaborative staff
(restorative justice, parent education, recreational programs)
• Law enforcement
• Community support/case advocate
• Volunteers

The case plan will include the identification of issues and an action plan for the minor and his or her parents and siblings. The action plan for the minor will focus on three general areas with the specific action steps tailored to the needs of the minor. These include
1. Community safety
2. Accountability
3. Competency development

The action plan for the parents will focus on family strengthening by reducing or eliminating:
1. The issues that impede the parents' ability to provide adequate supervision and control
2. Criminal family influence
3. The potential for family violence
4. Sources of family stress (e.g., substance abuse, lack of employment, illness, marital discord, etc.)

The action plan for the siblings will focus on:
1. Competency development
2. Health issues
3. Mental health issues
4. Education issues

Case Supervision

Control group: Based on the case classification, the DPO will establish regular contacts with the minor and family. The following are the minimum contact standards for cases based on their Risk/Needs classification:

High cases: 2 face to face contacts per month
Medium cases: 1 face to face contact per month
Low cases: 1 face to face contact every 90 days
Institutional commitments: No contact until pending release

Experimental group (8% Early Intervention Program): The DPO
serves the role of case manager for the entire family. The
following are the minimum and ideal DPO contact standards for
cases supervised by the 8% Early Intervention Program
regardless of case classification level (i.e., High, Medium or
Low) to monitor the implementation of the case plan for the
minor and family:

	Minimum	Ideal
Field	1X per week	2X per week
Parent	1X per week	2X per week
	2X per month phone	4X per month
	2X per month home	4X per month
School	Daily if at YFRC	Same
	2-4X per month if off-site	4X per month
Home	1 or 2X per week	2X per week
Office	1X per month	2X per month
Juvenile institutions		
JH or YGC	2X per month	2 x per month
JYC or LP	1X per month	1 x per month
	1 phone contact	1 phone contact

In order to implement the action, a service plan will be
developed for the minor and his/her family. The Service Plan
will include some or all of the following program components:

1. Education: Each minor will be enrolled in a school
   program that best meets his or her needs and will be
   referred for appropriate diagnostic services if
   questions arise about educational needs:
   • Comprehensive school
   • Alternative education
   • Private school
   • Independent Study
   • Day school program provided at the Youth and
     Family Resource Center by the Department of
     Education; transportation provided by Deputy
     Probation Counselors
   • Tutoring
   • Special services

2. Behavioral health (mental health, drug and alcohol
   abuse and mental functioning): Assessment of
   probation youth and family with appropriate follow-up
   services/program linkages, as indicated.

3. Competency development: Probation Counselors and Community Resource collaborative staff will provide programming in the following areas:
   - Independent living skills: vocational readiness, household management, health and hygiene, acquisition of proper documentation (i.e., social security number and California state identification), familiarization with public transportation, budgeting, bank checking account management, and job seeking.
   - Social skills and gang resistance skills: basic social and conversation skills, problem solving skills, recreation skills, and peer resistance skills.
   - Development of prosocial values and attachment to conventional institutions through development of a positive peer culture: daily group meetings at the Youth and Family Resource Center which provide a forum to confront delinquent values and for accountability for past behavior, and to help the minors gain an understanding of the ramifications and consequences of their behavior for themselves, their families, and their victims.
   - Substance abuse: an 18-week substance abuse curriculum will be made available to minors and families through daily groups and specially scheduled classes.

4. Accountability: All Youth and Family Resource Center staff will work together as a team at the center to assist the minor in developing prosocial values and holding the minor accountable for his/her behavior. In addition to the group counseling described above, the Community Resource Collaborative will coordinate activities with community-based organizations to ensure that minors in the program participate in work experiences that are restorative to the community. The minor may also be involved in work activities that permit him/her to pay restitution, if appropriate.

5. Recreational, cultural and social activities: Probation Counselors and Community Resource Collaborative staff will develop and supervise appropriate physical education and recreational activities for minors who attend the Youth and Family Resource Center. They

will also provide outings on a regular basis and will organize open houses, family picnics, and other activities designed to encourage the relationship building between the minor and his/her family.

6. Parent Education and Parent Support Groups: The Community Resource Collaborative will provide a parent education program that will meet at least bimonthly. The program will employ the STEP-Teen curriculum and will continue to recycle through the curriculum so that there will continuously be points of entry for newly admitted families. YFRC staff will provide family counseling on a regular basis both at the Youth and Family Resource Center and in the home.

7. Reducing Family Stressors: Families may be experiencing stress for a number of reasons (financial problems, medical problems, mental health problems, marital problems, etc.). As Youth and Family Resource Center staff become aware of these issues, families will receive services or be linked to the appropriate community-based resource. This may include

- Family preservation services, such as intensive in-home intervention
- Mental health services
- Health care education, assessment, intervention, and referral services provided by the American Academy of Pediatrics and the Health Care Agency
- Drug/alcohol abuse services provided by staff from the Health Care Agency
- Financial aid, emergency shelter, and other social services
- Educational assessment and services
- Employment services
- Other services, such as domestic violence counseling

Case Reassessment

Both experimental and control groups will complete a full reassessment of their cases at 6 month intervals. This reassessment will include:

> Risk/needs assessment
> Family assessment
> Case plan

Monitoring Monthly Service Delivery

Service delivery for both experimental and control cases will be monitored on a monthly basis through the submission of existing routine departmental service activity summaries and service record forms. These include:

> DPO supervision logs noting contacts provided for each case
> Monthly service summaries provided by service providers
> School records on attendance and behavior

Appendix E

Youth and Family Resource Center
Cost Components

Average daily on-site population	60 youth
Average number of youth and families served per year	100 youth and families
Average family size	5

Probation staff   **$600,000**
   1 Supervising Probation Officer
   4 Deputy Probation Officers
   6 Deputy Probation Counselors
   1 Information Processing Technician

Behavioral Health Services   **$250,000**
(Mental health, alcohol and drug abuse)

In-home Family Intervention Services   **$100,000**

Resource Collaborative Services   **$140,000**
(parent education, teen parenting, restorative justice and
recreational/cultural/social.)

Health Care Education, Screening and Follow-up   **$100,000**
Linkage Services

Building Lease   **$140,000**
(10,000 square feet: reception, 4 classrooms, conference
room, multi-purpose room, offices for multidisciplinary
staff, kitchen, and storage areas.)

Van Maintenance   **$20,000**
   2 vans

Other Program Expenses   **$50,000**
   Staff training
   Food
   Equipment
   Special activities

                                    Total   **$1,400,000**

Note: Individual component costs will vary by community and jurisdiction. The costs presented
here reflect start-up costs. Ongoing costs may be reduced through state and federal cost-
sharing and through increased community support. The costs shown here do not reflect one-
time expenses, such as the purchase of vans, furniture, or computers.

AUTHOR'S NOTE: The author prepared this chart for other jurisdictions
which have requested cost information on Orange County's program model.

Appendix F

The Repeat Offender Prevention Project
Summary of Program Evaluation Design

Program Goals and Objectives

The primary goal of the Repeat Offender Prevention Program (ROPP) is to break the escalating pattern of criminal and anti-social behavior that leads to chronic delinquency and, too often, criminal careers. This goal will be accomplished through the provision of support services that are designed to strengthen the family's ability to provide adequate supervision, structure and support for their children and also by providing minors with opportunities to develop skills and competencies that will enable them to lead a successful, law-abiding lifestyle.

Sample Selection

Most juvenile referrals to the Probation Department are pre-screened by Probation Intake staff to determine their potential availability for the program. Following wardship declaration, all eligible cases are forwarded to the supervisor of the ROPP for further screening and evaluation. Those cases that are determined to meet the selection criteria will, at this point, be reviewed by departmental research staff, who will assign each case to either the experimental or control group.

The two sample groups will be built as new wards are added to the caseloads. Sample cases will therefore have varying lengths of stay un-

---

AUTHOR'S NOTE: This summary was prepared as an attachment to the Orange County Probation Department's contract with the California Board of Corrections for Repeat Offender Prevention Project funding. The design document has been updated to reflect minor changes since project implementation.

der either form of supervision. By the end of the grant-funding period (June 2001), we will have 18-month comparative data for 85 to 90 youths, 12-month comparative data for 100 to 105 youths, and six-month comparative data for 120 to 125 youths assigned to the experimental and control groups, respectively.

Process Evaluation

The Orange County Repeat Offender Prevention Program has been designed to provide an enriched level of assessment and intervention services to both the minor and his or her family. It will be important to determine whether the type, frequency and quality of service provided by the program is demonstrably different from that provided through routine probation supervision.

Two sources of information will be used for process comparison:

1. The supervision case plan (updated every 90 days), which identifies the primary program components for both minor and family in relation to specific community security, offender accountability and competency development requirements.

2. A standardized Case Tracking form, which records services provided during each program month.

Outcome Evaluation

If the program goals can be successfully achieved, the following outcomes are expected to occur more for ROPP minors rather than the control group cases. In terms of short-term outcomes:

- Improvements in the number of days of school attendance

- Improvements in grades

- More education (course) credits earned

- Fewer behavioral incidents (suspensions/expulsions)

- More parental involvement in program — case conferences, contacts with the probation officer, involvement in community resources, participation in parent education, support groups and parent satisfaction ratings

- Minor involved in more pro-social activities – classes completed, community service hours performed, restitution paid

- Reductions in gang association or involvement – compliance with gang terms, fewer subsequent gang-related crimes

- Reductions in runaway or stealing behavior – fewer subsequent incidents

• Reduced use of alcohol or drugs – fewer positive tests and fewer subsequent drug-related crimes

With these short-term outcomes achieved, the following long-term results should follow:

• Fewer new law violations

• Fewer court appearances

• Fewer custody days

• Fewer minors who become adult offenders

A four-person Research Advisory Group has been established to oversee the internal evaluation being conducted by the Research unit of the Orange County Probation Department. This group also provides assistance to the entire statewide ROPP project to improve the consistency of the statewide research effort. The advisory group consists of

• Dr. James Austin, George Washington University

• Susan Turner, RAND Corporation

• Dr. Malcolm Klein, University of Southern California

• Dr. Jill Rosenbaum, California State University, Fullerton

Two-day meetings have been scheduled and will continue through FY 00-01 on a semi-annual basis with Orange as the host county. The Research Advisory Group will also review and comment on Orange County's final ROPP report to the Board of Corrections at the end of this project.

The final research evaluation report shall describe the conduct and findings of all process and outcome evaluation activities, shall comport with the research design and evaluation requirements of WIC Section 749, and shall describe the following in sufficient detail to permit replication of the research by other interested parties:

1. Research subjects

2. Research design (including identification and method of random assignment of research subjects per WIC Section 746)

3. The nature and extent of treatment interventions (for both control and treatment groups, to include required treatment modalities per WIC Section 747, and key intervention strategies per WIC Section 748)

4. Program evaluation measures

5. All other dependent and independent variables (including those in the common database adopted by all counties participating in the ROPP)

6. Data analysis procedures

The format of the report shall include the following sections:

1. Background information
2. Hypotheses
3. Methodology
4. Results
5. Discussion
6. Summary and conclusions

Copies of all data collection instruments (excluding those covered by copyright protection) shall be attached to the report.

References

Battin, S., Hill, K. G., Hawkins, J. P., Catalano, R. F. & Abbott, R. (1996). Testing gang membership and association with anti-social peers as independent predictors of social behavior. Paper presented at the annual meeting of the American Society of Criminology, Chicago.

Capizzi, M., Cook, J. I. & Schumacher, M. (1995 Fall). The TARGET model: A new approach to the prosecution of gang cases. The Prosecutor, 18-21.

Cohen, B. (1969). The delinquency of gangs and spontaneous groups. In T. Sellin & M. D. Wolfgang, (Eds.), Delinquency; Selected studies. New York: John Wiley.

Cohen, M. A. (1998), The monetary value of saving a high-risk youth. Journal of Quantitative Criminology, 14, 5-33.

Early childhood and brain development – CII speaks with Dr. Bruce Perry and Robin Karr-Morse regarding the damage of abuse and neglect, The CII Forum, Children's Institute International (CII) (1999, Winter).

Fagan, J. (1990). Social processes of delinquency and drug use among urban gangs. In C. R. Huff, (Ed.). Gangs in America. Newbury Park, CA: Sage.

Farrington, D., & Hawkins, D. (1991). Predicting participation, early onset and later persistence in officially recorded offending. Criminal Behavior and Mental Health, 1, 1-33.

Gendreau, P. (1993, November). The principles of effective intervention with offenders. Paper presented at the International Association of Residential and Community Alternatives, Philadelphia.

Greenwood, P. (1992). Reforming California's approach to delinquent and high-risk youth. In J. Steinberg, D. Lyon, and M. Varana (Eds.), Urban America: Policy choices for Los Angeles and the nation. Santa Monica, CA: RAND.

Hamperin, D., Schuster, R., Dinitz, S., & Conrad, J. (1978). The violent few, a study of dangerous juvenile offenders. Lexington, MA: Lexington Books.

Huizinga, D. (1997). Gangs and the volume of crime. Paper presented at the annual meeting of the Western Society of Criminology, Honolulu, HI.

Huizinga, D., Esbensen, F., & Weiher, A. (1991). Are there multiple pathways to delinquency? Journal of Criminal Law and Criminology, 82, 83-118.

Huizinga, D., & Jakob-Chien, C. (1998). The contemporaneous co-occurrence of serious violent offending and other problem behavior. In R. Loeber & D. P. Farrington (Eds.), Serious, violent juvenile offenders: Risk factors and successful interventions, (pp. 47-67). Thousand Oaks, CA: Sage.

Huizinga, D., Loeber, R. & Thornberry, T. (1993). Urban delinquency and substance abuse. Washington, DC: U.S. Department of Justice, Office of Juvenile Justice and Delinquency Prevention.

Kelly, B., Thornberry, T. & Smith, C. (1997). In the wake of childhood maltreatment. Washington, DC: U.S. Department of Justice, Office of Juvenile Justice and Delinquency Prevention.

Klein, M. W. , Gordon, M. A. & Maxson, C. L. (1989). Street gang violence. In N. A. Weiner &, M. E. Wolfgang (Eds.), Violent crime, violent criminals. Newbury Park, CA: Sage.

Klein, M. W., Gordon, M. A. & Maxson, C. L. (1986). The impact of police investigation on police-reported rates of gang and non-gang homicides. Criminology, 24, 489-512.

Kumpfer, K. (1993). Strengthening America's families: Promising parenting strategies for delinquency prevention. Washington, DC: U.S. Department of Justice, Office of Juvenile Justice and Delinquency Prevention.

Kurz, G. A. and Moore, L. E. (1994). "The 8% problem": Chronic juvenile offender recidivism, Santa Ana, CA. Orange County Probation Department.

Lipsey, M. W. (1995). What do we learn from 400 research studies on the effectiveness of treatment with juvenile delinquents? In J. McGuire, J. (Ed.), What works? Reducing re-offending (pp. 63-78),New York: John Wiley.

Lipsey, M. W. and Wilson, D. B. (1998). Effective interventions with serious juvenile offenders: A synthesis of research. In R. Loeber & D.P. Farrington (Eds.), Serious and violent juvenile offenders: Risk factors and successful interventions (pp. 313-345). Thousand Oaks, CA: Sage.

Loeber, R., & Stouthamer-Loeber, M. (1986). Family factors as correlates and predictors of juvenile conduct problems and delinquency. In N. Morris & M. Tonry, (Eds.), Crime and justice: Annual review of research. Chicago: University of Chicago Press.

Maloney, D., Romig, D., & Armstrong, T. (1988). Juvenile Probation: The balanced approach. Juvenile and Family Court Journal. 39 (3).

McCord, J. (1991). Family relationships, juvenile delinquency, and adult criminality. Criminology, 29(3), 557-580.

Minty, B. (1988). Public care or distorted family relationships: The antecedents of violent crime. Howard Journal, 27(3), 172-187.

Mulvey, E., & LaRosa, J., Jr., (1986). Delinquency cessation and adolescent development: Preliminary data." American Journal of Orthopsychiatry, 56(2), 212-224.

Nagin, D., & Farrington, D. (1992). The onset and persistence of offending. Criminology, 30, 501-523.

Richardson, G., Neiger, B., Jensen, S., & Kumpfer, K. (1990). The resiliency model. Health Education, 21, 33-39.

Rutter, M. (1987a). Continuities and discontinuities from infancy. In J. Osotsky, (Ed.), Handbook on infant development (2nd ed.). New York: John Wiley.

Rutter, M. (1987b). Early sources of security and competence. In J. S. Bruner & A. Garten (Eds.), Human growth and development. London: Oxford University Press.

Rutter, M. (1990). Psychosocial resilience and protective mechanisms. (pp. 316-331). New York: American Orthopsychiatric Association.

Rutter, M., & Quinton, D. (1984). Long-term follow-up of women institutionalized in childhood. Factors promoting good functioning in adult life. Journal of Developmental Psychology, 18, 225-234.

Shannon, L. (1988). Criminal career continuity: Its social context, New York: Human Sciences Press.

Stewart, D., (1996), The 8% solution: Medical intervention (CATCH planning grant final report). American Academy of Pediatrics, Orange, CA.

Strasburg, P. (1978) Violent delinquents. Report to the Ford Foundation from the Vera Institute of Justice. New York: Monarch Press.

Thornberry, T. F. (1996). The contribution of gang members to the volume of delinquency. Fact sheet prepared for the U.S. Department of Justice, Office of Juvenile Justice and Delinquency Prevention, Washington DC.

Werner, E. (1986). Resilient offspring of alcoholics: A longitudinal study from birth to age 18. Journal of Studies of Alcoholism, 47, 34-40.

Wilson, J. J. & Howell, J. C. (1993). A comprehensive strategy for serious, violent and chronic juvenile offenders: A program summary. U.S. Department of Justice, Office of Juvenile Justice and Delinquency Prevention, Washington DC.

Wilson, J. Q., & Hernstein, R. (1985). Crime and human nature. New York: Simon & Schuster.

Wolfgang, M. E., Figlio, R. M. & Sellin, T. (1972). Delinquency in a birth cohort. Chicago: University of Chicago Press.

Wolfgang, M. E., Thornberry, T. P. & Figlio, R. M. (1987). From boy to man, from delinquency to crime. Chicago: University of Chicago Press.

Wright, K., & Wright, K. (1992). Family life and delinquency and crime: A policymakers' guide to the literature. Washington, DC: U.S. Department of Justice, Office of Juvenile Justice and Delinquency Prevention.

About the Authors

Gwen A. Kurz is Director of Program Support and Research for the Orange County (California) Probation Department and has worked in the field of criminal justice research for more than 25 years. She is a past president and current board member of the Association for Criminal Justice Research (California) and a recognized expert in juvenile offender risk assessment. She was the principal investigator for a longitudinal research project entitled, The 8% Problem: Chronic Juvenile Offender Recidivism. She designed and is currently testing an early intervention program model aimed at preventing serious, chronic offending – the 8% Problem Solution.

Michael A. Schumacher, PhD, has served as the Chief Probation Officer in Orange County, California, since 1979 and has worked in the field of corrections for more than 29 years. The department he oversees employs more than 1,500 people, has an annual budget of $93 million, operates five institutions for juvenile offenders, and is responsible for nearly 21,000 adult and juvenile offenders. He has served gubernatorial appointments on the California Council on Criminal Justice, the Robert E. Presley Institute for Corrections, Research, and Training, and on the Commission for Revision of the Juvenile Court Law. He is currently the Legislative Chairperson for the Chief Probation Officers of California (CPOC) and is a former president of CPOC and of the California Probation, Parole, and Correctional Association. Dr. Schumacher early recognized the value of the 8% Problem research. He secured county and state support for funding to make the 8% Solution a reality.